HOW TO ACHIEVE THE EVERY CHILD MATTERS STANDARDS: A PRACTICAL GUIDE

How to Achieve the Every Child Matters Standards: A Practical Guide

Rita Cheminais

Los Angeles • London • New Delhi • Singapore

First published 2007
Reprinted 2008

SAGE Publications Ltd
1 Oliver's Yard
55 City Road
London EC1Y 1SP

SAGE Publications Inc
2455 Teller Road
Thousand Oaks, California 91320

SAGE Publications India Pvt Ltd
B 1/11 Mohan Cooperative Industrial Area
Mathura Road
New Delhi 110 044

SAGE Publications Asia – Pacific Pte Ltd
33 Pekin Street #02-01
Far East Square
Singapore 048763

Library of Congress Control Number: 2007935603

British Library Cataloguing in Publication Data
A catalogue record for this book is available from the British Library

ISBN-978-1-4129-4815-9
ISBN-978-1-4129-4816-6 (pbk)

Typeset by Pantek Arts Ltd, Maidstone, Kent
Printed in Great Britain by Cromwell Press Ltd, Trowbridge, Wiltshire
Printed on paper from sustainable resources

CONTENTS

Contents of accompanying CD

The CD includes document files in Microsoft® Word versions of the tables and templates that are featured throughout this resource.

Acrobat Reader version 3 or higher is required to view and print the relevant PDF documents from the CD, which are in A4 format.

CHAPTER 1 – CD EXAMPLES

- Every Child Matters Standards Information Brochure
- Every Child Matters Standards PowerPoint Presentation
- Every Child Matters Model Contract of Agreement

CHAPTER 2 – CD EXAMPLES

- Every Child Matters Improvement Planning and Self-evaluation Cycle

CHAPTER 3 – CD EXAMPLES

- Every Child Matters Standards Initial Audit Framework
- Every Child Matters Standards Action Plan Template

CHAPTER 4 – CD EXAMPLES

- Every Child Matters Portfolio of Evidence Checklists

CHAPTER 5 – CD EXAMPLES

- Every Child Matters Twelve Standard Descriptors
- Every Child Matress Standards Evidence Tables

CHAPTER 6 – CD EXAMPLES

- Every Child Matters Standards Monitoring and Evaluation Checklist
- Every Child Matters Standards Reflection and Review Questionnaire
- Every Child Matters Standards Model Award Certificate

About the Author

Rita Cheminais is a leading expert in the fields of inclusion, Every Child Matters and special educational needs (SEN) in mainstream primary, secondary and special schools, and in local authority Children's Services. With a background as a teacher, a SEN Coordinator, an OFSTED Inspector, and a Senior Local Authority Adviser, Rita has thirty-two years' practical experience.

She is a prolific writer and respected author of journal articles and books in the field of inclusion, Every Child Matters and SEN. Rita speaks regularly at national conferences and was one of the three 'Ask the Experts' participating in the Becta NGfL live online national inclusion conference in 2003.

For more details about Rita's consultancy work to support schools in working towards achieving the Every Child Matters Standards Award visit her website www.ecm-solutions.org.uk

Dedication

To my wonderful mother, Joan Cheminais, who has displayed increasing patience with me over endless weekends and holidays during the writing of this book, and who, despite her own painful illness, continues to support and encourage me throughout my working life. Thank you for being my 'rock' and making it all worthwhile.

Acknowledgements

The inspiration for this book came from an idea I shared with delegates during my seminar presentation at a recent national SEN conference in London. It is also the result of my consultations with all the dedicated, dynamic and innovative school leaders, heads of children's centres and PRUs, inclusion managers and SENCOs I have had the privilege to work with, who have put my ideas and advice into practice and who have made a positive difference to the learning and well-being outcomes for children and young people within their learning communities.

I wish to thank Ian Smith, Executive Director of Tameside Services for Children and Young People, Jim Taylor, Director of Education in Tameside, Steve Noble, Head of the School Improvement Service in Tameside, and all the other wonderful and inspiring school improvement, SEN and inclusion colleagues I work with in Tameside, who continue to encourage and support my creative thinking.

My special thanks go to Jude Bowen, Senior Commissioning Editor, and Katie Metzler, Assistant Editor, at Paul Chapman Publishing, for their advice and support in making this book a reality, and for believing in my ideas.

Introduction

The book will offer a consistent approach to supporting and complementing the processes of self-evaluation and improvement planning in a range of educational settings to meet the Every Child Matters outcome requirements for children and young people, aligned with the Ofsted inspection and other national standard requirements.

The Every Child Matters (ECM) Change for Children programme is a ten-year evolving strategy. There is a continual volume of information available on the Every Child Matters website *www.everychildmatters.gov.uk* – which at times can be overwhelming – to support a range of educational settings and local authority Children's Services in implementing this huge change agenda and equipping a skilled Children's Workforce.

This resource aims to enable local authorities in partnership with a range of educational settings which includes:

- early years settings

- mainstream and special schools in the primary and secondary phase

- pupil referral units

- children's centres

- sixth form and FE colleges

to work towards achieving the Every Child Matters Standards by fully meeting the twelve Standard evidence descriptors which are consistent with government legislation and guidance and align with an educational setting's own self-evaluation and improvement planning processes.

The Every Child Matters Standards are focused on enabling educational settings to gather secure and telling evidence in order to demonstrate and gain recognition for the impact of their actions, initiatives and interventions on the personalised learning and well-being outcomes for children and young people. It reflects and meets the expectations of Ofsted inspections, and complements other Quality Mark processes, e.g. the Basic Skills Quality Mark, Investors in People, Healthy School Award, Inclusion Quality Mark and the Quality in Extended Schools Award scheme.

The Every Child Matters Standards self-evaluation process supports educational settings in ensuring children and young people achieve their optimum potential, by adopting a holistic approach to learning and well-being, both of which are synonymous and go hand-in-hand with improving and achieving better outcomes for all. It also helps to bring the inclusion and standards agendas together to become complementary rather than competing priorities.

Educational settings that are members of Education Improvement Partnerships and Networked Learning Communities or Federations can utilise the Every Child Matters Standards to improve ECM policy and practice not only within their own organisation, but together, with other local partners, across a cluster of settings and extended services.

External moderation, assessment and validation commissioned from a local authority, a reputable accreditation agency or organisation, or from a higher education institution acting as a 'critical friend', will be a necessary requirement to enable any educational setting or cluster to achieve external recognition and an award certificate for meeting all the Every Child Matters Standards. The certificate remains valid for three years and can be renewed thereafter.

How to use this book

This book with accompanying CD is designed to support all those involved in leading and evaluating the Every Child Matters well-being outcomes in a range of educational settings. The resource enables:

- schools
- PRUs
- children's centres
- sixth-form and FE colleges

to gather a range of telling evidence that will contribute to informing the Ofsted Self-Evaluation Form (SEF) and local authority children's services accountability processes about how they are improving the personalised learning and well-being outcomes for children, young people and their families within their local learning community.

It supports the development of a portfolio of evidence for the Every Child Matters outcomes which can be utilised to disseminate good practice across the local authority's educational settings, as well as contributing to an individual setting achieving the Every Child Matters Standards.

Some qualitative evidence related to the Every Child Matters five outcomes can be subjective and relate to individual 'real' stories, which often cannot be demonstrated on an Ofsted SEF. These 'real' stories, as case studies of better outcomes for individual or cohorts of vulnerable children and young people with additional needs, can be included within a portfolio of evidence, providing they are anonymous in accordance with the data protection and information-sharing protocols.

The journey and time scale towards achieving the Every Child Matters Standards is determined by the context and the capacity of the individual setting or cluster group. This resource will enable each educational setting or cluster to know what evidence is required as they travel along the Every Child Matters journey of self-evaluation, by using the detailed evidence descriptors, within each of the twelve Standards to cross-check their current position. The ECM Standards model of self-evaluation will also help to identify priority areas in relation to Every Child Matters outcomes requiring further development and improvement.

Whatever the outcome for the educational setting undertaking the ECM Standards process, the collaborative productive partnerships and team work established throughout the self-evaluation process will contribute immensely to achieving better outcomes for all stakeholders involved, i.e. children and young people, parents and carers, teaching and non-teaching staff, governors, partners from the local community, external multi-agencies and voluntary sector independent organisations.

Overall, this valuable and essential resource will provide a meaningful and relevant evidence base grounded in real practice for internal and external use which will enhance reflection and respond appropriately to the national expectations of the Every Child Matters change for children agenda. Enjoy working through the ECM Standards process in achieving your ultimate goal of securing better outcomes for children and young people.

CHAPTER 1

The Every Child Matters Standards

This chapter introduces the Every Child Matters Standards. It explains:

■ the concept and principles of the Every Child Matters Standards;

■ where and when to utilise the Every Child Matters Standards;

■ the advantages of engaging in the Every Child Matters Standards Award process;

■ the role of the Every Child Matters external assessors.

The concept of the Every Child Matters Standards

The ECM Standards originated from the need for educational settings to gain external recognition for their ECM policy and practice beyond the Ofsted inspection process, and to be able to demonstrate to a range of stakeholders that they are responding appropriately to the government's Every Child Matters Change for Children strategy.

When the government published the Green Paper entitled *Every Child Matters* in 2003, and their *Five Year Strategy for Children and Learners* a year later, they made explicit in these documents their vision and expectation that educational settings have an important role to play, as a universal service provider themselves, to improve the educational achievement, quality of life and well-being outcomes for children and young people.

The ECM Standards align closely with the Ofsted inspection framework self-evaluation process. They are consistent with central and local government legislation related to Every Child Matters. They enable educational settings to gather harder quantitative ECM outcomes data and telling qualitative evidence in order to demonstrate the impact of actions and extended service provision on improving the learning and ECM well-being outcomes for children and young people.

Every Child Matters acknowledges that children and young people cannot learn effectively if they do not feel safe, healthy or happy, and that learning and well-being go hand in hand. Clearly, educational settings are not solely responsible for improving Every Child Matters outcomes. Together, in collaboration with service users (children, young people and their families) and other statutory agencies, including voluntary and community sector partners, they develop and deliver accessible personalised services and wraparound care on, or near the site of the educational setting, to improve personalised learning and the ECM outcomes for children and young people.

The *2020 Vision Report on Teaching and Learning* indicated that:

> Society's aspirations for learners are expressed in the outcomes of the Every Child Matters framework . . . Increased collaboration, as part of the Every Child Matters agenda, creates a climate in which personalisation can take place.

> (DfES, 2007: 5 and 10)

Guiding principles

The following guiding principles provide a baseline of entry criteria for commencing on the Every Child Matters Standards self-evaluation process.

- The educational setting's leader has shared their passion, enthusiasm and vision for Every Child Matters with key stakeholders.

- An Every Child Matters visioning and awareness raising event has already taken place within the educational setting, which has informed stakeholders of the bigger picture.

- There is an ethos of openness, consultation, participation and shared ownership for Every Child Matters in existence among stakeholders.

- The well-being of children/young people and staff within the educational setting is important and valued.

- A collaborative culture exists within a secure learning community, which promotes research, reflection, creativity and innovation for Every Child Matters.

- The educational setting takes the wider community view for Every Child Matters and networks with other settings, services and organisations.

- There is a designated senior staff member responsible for leading and overseeing the ECM Standards process within the educational setting.

- A core team of staff has been established within the educational setting, with clear roles and responsibilities for intelligent accountability in gathering evidence for the twelve ECM standards.

- A contract, outlining the terms of reference for the ECM Standards Award scheme has been explained, agreed and signed by the leader of the educational setting and a representative/assessor from the ECM Standards Team.

Where the Every Child Matters Standards can be utilised

The ECM Standards self-evaluation process will enable any educational setting, whether it be an early years setting, a children's centre, a special school, a mainstream school in the primary and secondary phase with or without a resourced provision, a pupil referral unit (PRU), or a sixth-form/FE college, in partnership with other service providers, to successfully meet the demands and expectations of the Every Child Matters agenda, as part of their everyday practice.

When to work towards achieving the Every Child Matters Standards

When it is most appropriate for an educational setting to begin to engage with the ECM Standards process is very much dependent on their current context and the starting point from which the setting is approaching the Every Child Matters change for children programme. Chapter 2 provides more detail about the stages an educational setting needs to go through in order to achieve the ECM Standards.

Table 1.1 indicates when it is, and is not, appropriate to proceed along the journey towards achieving the ECM Standards.

Table 1.1 Appropriateness as to when to engage in the ECM Standards Award

When it is NOT appropriate to participate in the ECM Standards Award	When it IS appropriate to participate in the ECM Standards Award
■ A setting is facing closure	■ Stakeholders within an educational setting have the 'will' to meet the ECM change for children agenda
■ A setting is going through an amalgamation	■ Staff in the setting have the capacity to deliver and respond to the ECM strategy
■ A setting is currently involved in a new building project	■ The setting is already successfully delivering wraparound care and extended services
■ A school or PRU is in Special Measures, as categorised following an Ofsted inspection	■ The setting's policy and practice in ECM outcomes was judged by Ofsted to be good or outstanding

Although the ECM Standards, as a self-evaluation process, requires commitment, it is a process that is manageable, rewarding and owned by all participants within the educational setting.

The advantages of undertaking the ECM Standards Award process

The advantages of participating in the ECM Standards self-assessment process are as follows:

- The structure of the ECM Standards framework meets the expectations of a twenty-first century education system and Children's Workforce.

- The ECM Standards framework aligns with Ofsted inspection requirements and other national quality standards.

- The process towards achieving the ECM Standards Award engages a range of stakeholders as active participants.

- The ECM Standards support capacity building for Every Child Matters within and across a range of educational settings.

- The dissemination and sharing of best ECM practice is promoted.

- There is the potential for educational settings to be offered external recognition for their good quality Every Child Matters policy and practice, through the award of the ECM Standards Certificate.

Every Child Matters Standards assessors

The assessors who make up the ECM Standards quality assurance team can be any of the following:

- local authority and independent school improvement advisers and inspectors;

- educational psychologists;

- advisory or consultant teachers;

- advanced skills teachers or excellent teachers;

- principals/deputy principals from FE/sixth-form colleges, headteachers/deputy headteachers from schools, and heads from PRUs, children's centres and early years settings;

- senior lecturers from higher education institutions;

- independent educational consultants;

- senior practitioners from health and social services with an education background.

Assessors require substantial experience and knowledge which cover:

- the phase of educational setting they are assessing;

- Every Child Matters policy and practice;

- using the ECM Standards Framework;

- improvement planning;

- self-evaluation;

- data analysis, leadership and management;

- personalised learning;

- assessment for learning;

- inclusion.

Assessors need to allocate at least five days as a minimum per educational setting over the agreed period of time for achieving the ECM Standards Award. This will cover:

- scrutiny of ECM documentary evidence;

- on-site visits to observe and research ECM practice and provision first-hand;

- report writing;

- telephone and/or e-mail advice, support and guidance;

- INSET delivery.

Moderation between assessors of the ECM Standards evidence gathered from educational settings ensures a fair, consistent and valid approach to assessment and quality assurance is adopted.

The role of the ECM Standards assessor should be included in job descriptions. The income generated from undertaking the assessor role is ploughed back into the local authority, HE institution or educational settings budget, or to the commissioned independent company or organisation. ECM Standards assessors must ensure that their own continuing professional development relates to Every Child Matters and to their assessment role, and that it is kept up to date.

The members of an ECM Standards assessment team must be CRB-enhanced checked, as they will be gaining first-hand evidence from children and young people, during the final on-site assessment visit to educational settings.

Case study: ECM Standards Assessor final school assessment visit

Jane Wall is a full-time ECM Change and School Improvement Adviser working within a unitary local authority. She has agreed in advance with the headteacher of Investa Community Primary School the planned programme for the final assessment day visit to the school.

Investa Community Primary School is not one of her link schools, but she has obtained an initial view of the school's context and their work to date on Every Child Matters from an analysis of data and the school's ECM Standards portfolio of evidence which was submitted in advance of the planned visit.

Tuesday morning, Jane arrives at the school for 8.30 a.m. where she is welcomed by the school receptionist and the headteacher. There are no changes to the agreed programme for the day's visit.

8.40 – 9.30   Focused discussion with the headteacher and deputy headteacher leading and overseeing the ECM Standards process throughout the school, and the Chair of Governors responsible for Every Child Matters. During discussions, Jane clarifies their views about the school's ECM strengths, the progress made in addressing the ECM priorities identified by initial audit and on the action plan, and the progress they consider to have been made in improving the ECM outcomes for pupils.

9.30 – 10.00   Learning walk around the school, escorted by two pupil representatives from the School Council, with an opportunity to ask the pupils questions about anything observed during the tour related to ECM outcomes.

10.00 – 10.30 Focused discussion with a small group of four parents, two of whom are parent governors and two who assist in the running of an after-school club.

Their views are sought about the impact of undertaking the ECM Standards Award process on pupil outcomes, which provides a useful cross-check with the earlier discussion with the leadership team and the chair of governors.

10.30 – 11.00 Meeting with pupil ECM class representatives, accompanied by a teaching assistant. Focused discussion seeks the children's views about their awareness of the ECM outcomes, which activities or aspects of school life have helped them to achieve better ECM outcomes and what else the school needs to do in order to make ECM outcomes even better for pupils.

11.00 – 11.20 Coffee break and time for Jane to reflect on the morning's discussions.

11.20 – 12.00 Jane observes snapshots of four lessons across the school:
Nursery, Reception, Year 2 and Year 5, accompanied by the deputy headteacher.

12.00 – 12.30 Lunch with pupils in the dining hall.

12.30 – 13.00 Jane observes snapshots of lunchtime clubs and outdoor playground activities.

13.10 – 13.40 Focused discussion with a small group of representative class teachers and teaching assistants who have responsibility for overseeing, monitoring and reviewing an ECM outcome, whole-school, to seek their views on the operational management of the ECM Standards process and the impact on pupil outcomes.

13.40 – 14.10 Meeting with a small group of non-teaching school support staff: site manager, mid-day supervisor, school cook and the school nurse. Jane seeks their views about the ECM outcomes, their role and contributions to improving the ECM outcomes for pupils within the school, and the impact of undertaking the ECM Standards Award on pupils, well-being.

14.10 – 14.30 Coffee break for Jane, giving her time to reflect on lunchtime observations and afternoon discussions with the staff and to form an overall view about the school's quality of ECM provision and the impact of this provision on pupils' outcomes.

14.30 – 15.00 Verbal feedback to the headteacher on findings from the day visit and from the ECM Standards portfolio of evidence documentation. Verbal confirmation is given to the headteacher as to whether the school has met the ECM Standards and achieved the Award, and if not, what the school needs to do to secure the Award at embedded level. Thanks are given to the headteacher for accommodating the visit, and to confirm that the headteacher will receive a full written assessment report in four weeks' time, confirming that the school has achieved the ECM Standards Award.

15.00 The ECM Standards Assessor Jane departs from the school.

Points to remember

When making a decision about when to commence the ECM Standards award process consider:

■ designating a member of the senior leadership team to take lead responsibility for overseeing the entire ECM Standards process;

■ establishing a core team of staff with sufficient time to gather the evidence required for each of the twelve ECM Standards;

■ securing the services of a credible external assessor.

How to achieve the Every Child Matters Standards

This chapter outlines the process of working towards achieving the Every Child Matters Standards. Using the analogy of a journey it covers:

■ the two routes that can be taken, based on the educational setting's context and current position with regard to implementing Every Child Matters;

■ the cycle of school improvement planning and self-evaluation underpinning the achievement of the Every Child Matters Standards Award;

■ the programme of support offered by the external ECM Standards assessor and the expectations at each stage of the assessment process.

Introduction

Educational settings will undoubtedly benefit immensely from working towards achieving the Every Child Matters Standards. The process of evidence gathering will enable the individual setting or cluster group of settings to focus on improving practice in relation to meeting the Every Child Matters five well-being outcome requirements. It will also provide the necessary checks and balances to support educational settings in implementing the Every Child Matters Change for Children programme.

Through offering the potential for external assessment and accreditation, the ECM Standards enable educational settings to gain recognition for their work and achievements in the area of Every Child Matters.

The route map

Educational settings working towards achieving the ECM Standards will be at varying stages in implementing the Every Child Matters change agenda. As a result of this factor, one of two routes can be adopted by the setting or cluster on their journey towards obtaining the ECM Standards Award.

Route 1

Route 1 is appropriate for those settings or clusters who consider they have already made a very good start in implementing ECM policy and provision. For example, they may be a full-service extended school or a children's centre, offering a good range of personalised learning opportunities, wraparound care and personalised services to children, young people and their families. If this is the case, then they will be well placed to work on gathering evidence on all twelve ECM Standards and to consider achieving the ECM Standards Award over a period of between one and two years.

Route 2

This second route is ideally suited to those educational settings or clusters who have only just begun to raise awareness about Every Child Matters with stakeholders, and who are still seeking to establish productive partnerships in order to extend and enhance personalised services and personalised learning opportunities. In such an instance, these educational settings would be well advised to work on no more than four ECM Standards within a period of twelve months, completing their evidence-gathering process covering all twelve Standards in three years.

Whichever route is selected for the journey towards achieving all the ECM Standards, they are both underpinned by the improvement planning and self-evaluation processes necessary to meet the requirements of an Ofsted inspection and a New Relationship with Schools single conversation with the School Improvement Partner (SIP).

Improvement planning, self-evaluation and Every Child Matters

Figure 2.1 illustrates the sequence of improvement planning and self-evaluation stages that are followed when working towards achieving the ECM Standards.

Stage 1 – Baseline current position: how are we doing with Every Child Matters?

An initial consultation with stakeholders and an audit is carried out using the ECM Standards Initial Audit Framework Summary to establish a baseline, which indicates current thinking, practice and progress within the educational setting or across the cluster, in relation to informing future Every Child Matters policy, planning and provision.

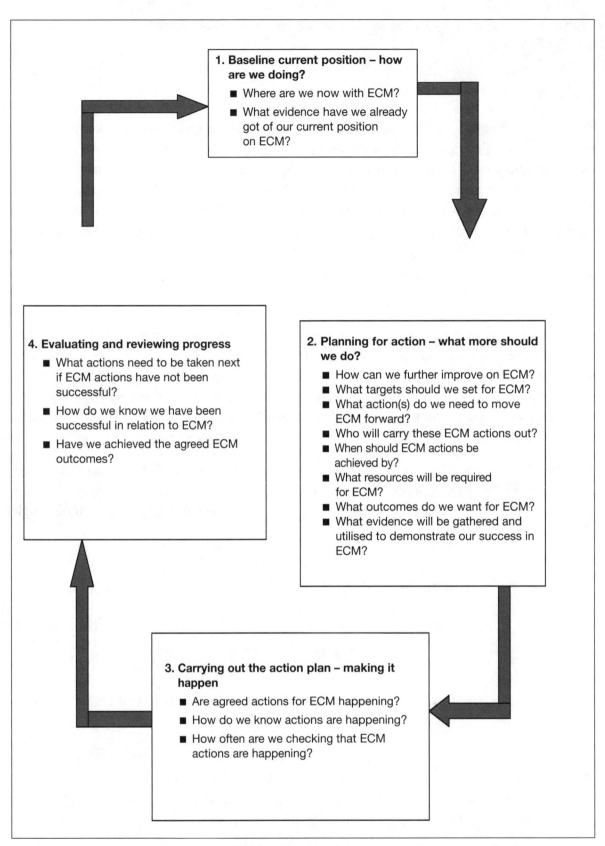

1. Baseline current position – how are we doing?

■ Where are we now with ECM?

■ What evidence have we already got of our current position on ECM?

4. Evaluating and reviewing progress

■ What actions need to be taken next if ECM actions have not been successful?

■ How do we know we have been successful in relation to ECM?

■ Have we achieved the agreed ECM outcomes?

2. Planning for action – what more should we do?

■ How can we further improve on ECM?

■ What targets should we set for ECM?

■ What action(s) do we need to move ECM forward?

■ Who will carry these ECM actions out?

■ When should ECM actions be achieved by?

■ What resources will be required for ECM?

■ What outcomes do we want for ECM?

■ What evidence will be gathered and utilised to demonstrate our success in ECM?

3. Carrying out the action plan – making it happen

■ Are agreed actions for ECM happening?

■ How do we know actions are happening?

■ How often are we checking that ECM actions are happening?

Figure 2.1 Improvement planning and self-evaluation underpinning the ECM Standards
(Adapted from Birmingham City Council Education Service, 2002: 11., © BBC.)

Stage 2: Planning for action – what more should we do for Every Child Matters?

This stage requires the ECM priorities identified from the audit requiring further development and improvement for the year, to be clarified in a plan of action which forms part of the educational setting's development plan.

Stage 3: Carrying out the action plan for Every Child Matters – making it happen

The senior manager responsible for overseeing Every Child Matters within the educational setting, along with the six or twelve key staff each responsible for leading, monitoring, evaluating and reviewing progress made in one or two of the twelve ECM standards, regularly check that agreed and planned actions take place. Evidence of the actions taken and of the progress made towards meeting the ECM priorities on the development plan, are fed back to the leadership team and the governing body or management board, as well as being included in the ECM portfolio of evidence.

Stage 4: Evaluating and reviewing progress for Every Child Matters

This stage of the process focuses on self-evaluation of Every Child Matters Standards, i.e. judging the impact of actions taken on the ECM well-being outcomes for children and young people. It will confirm, through the ongoing gathering of evidence, whether the educational setting or cluster has achieved the expected outcomes and met the success criteria in relation to the ECM priorities on the development plan. In addition, it will identify ECM strengths as well as areas for further improvement in Every Child Matters. This self-evaluation and review of progress will be recorded against the ECM Standards descriptors.

The process towards achieving the Every Child Matters Standards Award

In order to enable an educational setting to achieve the ECM Standards, one of two routes can be pursued.

Individual educational settings and the Every Child Matters Standards

Where a local authority or a higher education institution or any other external accreditation organisation have been commissioned as the external ECM Standards assessor, an individual educational setting can buy into the assessment scheme, which will provide:

- an initial visit by an external ECM Standards assessor who will outline and explain the process and procedures towards achieving the Standards Award to the setting's leadership team/leader, advise on ECM marketing and the action planning process and negotiate a contract for consultancy and support;

- an initial INSET session for staff and other key stakeholders in the educational setting/cluster on the ECM Standards process, explaining how to use the ECM Standards Framework;

- access to telephone support, and/or on-line support and e-mail conferencing from the ECM Standards Team;

- an interim visit from the external assessor to the educational setting in order to review progress towards meeting the criteria for each of the twelve ECM Standards and in meeting the ECM priorities set on the action plan/development plan;

- advice to the educational setting/cluster as to whether and when they are likely to be ready to be externally assessed for the ECM Standards Award;

- an allocated external assessor(s) from the ECM Standards Team who will request the ECM portfolio of evidence and other key accompanying ECM documentation two weeks before undertaking the on-site final ECM assessment visit;

- an agreed date for the day visit to the educational setting or cluster, with a programme outlining the first-hand evidence the external assessor wishes to collect, which can include observation of ECM practice and provision, interviews with key stakeholders and examples of children and young people's ECM achievements, including data analysis;

- four weeks following the on-site assessment visit, a full report from the assessor confirming success or otherwise in fully meeting all the twelve ECM Standards;

- an ECM Standards Certificate which will be awarded at a local authority or regional awards ceremony to the educational settings who successfully and fully meet all twelve ECM Standards.

Clusters and the Every Child Matters Standards

One educational setting within an Education Improvement Partnership (EIP), a federation, a cluster or a networked learning community, for example, will take a lead role in implementing the ECM Standards across a group of local educational settings, which may comprise a children's centre, a primary and secondary school, a special school and a pupil referral unit. Together, the group of educational settings can work towards achieving an ECM Cluster Standards Award, once external assessment and accreditation have been secured, following the same assessment process as for an individual setting.

Each setting within the cluster, EIP, federation or networked learning community would have to achieve the ECM Standards 1 and 2 at embedded level, and the other ten ECM Standards between them, across the settings. The eventual goal, however, would be for each individual educational setting within the cluster to achieve all twelve ECM Standards at embedded level.

Validity of the Every Child Matters Standards Award

Once an educational setting or cluster of settings has achieved the ECM Standards Award, this becomes valid for three years. After this three-year period the setting or cluster is recommended to undertake an ECM review and to reapply for a renewal external assessment from the ECM Standards Team. The same requirements have to be met as those undertaken for the first ECM Standards Award.

Points to remember

■ Giving external recognition for achievements in Every Child Matters outcomes is reliant on gathering in-depth telling evidence from a range of stakeholders, to present to an external ECM Standards assessor.

■ An individual setting, or a small group of educational settings in a cluster, will need to decide the length of time they judge to be reasonable in which to work towards achieving the ECM Standards award within a three-year period.

■ The ECM Standards assessment process readily fits into the regular improvement and self-evaluation annual cycle.

■ The ECM Standards external programme of support, monitoring and final assessment provides a robust quality assurance check, tailored to the context of the educational setting or cluster of settings.

CHAPTER 3

Undertaking the Every Child Matters Initial Standards Audit

This chapter describes in depth and provides the Every Child Matters Standards initial self-evaluation audit for educational settings to use in order to judge their current position at the start of the ongoing assessment process. It outlines:

■ the benefits of undertaking the Every Child Matters Standards audit;

■ the twelve aspects covered by the Every Child Matters Standards audit;

■ the steps to take in the Every Child Matters Standards audit process;

■ the production of an audit report of findings to inform the Every Child Matters Standards action plan.

Introduction

The Every Child Matters Standards Initial Audit Framework included in this chapter, which is also available on the accompanying CD as a Microsoft Word document, provides a self-evaluation audit tool for any educational setting to use in order to judge its current position in relation to Every Child Matters (ECM) policy and practice against the twelve ECM Standards evidence descriptors at three levels:

■ *Emergent* – in the early stages of development and 35 per cent met.

■ *Developing* – in progress and 70 per cent met.

■ *Embedded* – fully in place and 100 per cent met.

What aspects are covered by the Every Child Matters Standards?

The Every Child Matters Standards cover twelve aspects, which are aligned to the five ECM well-being outcomes. The twelve ECM Standards aspects are:

Standard 1:   Ethos

Standard 2:   Policy

Standard 3:   The Environment

Standard 4:   Leadership and Management

Standard 5:   Personalised Learning

Standard 6:   Curriculum Entitlement, Access and Choice

Standard 7:   Presence, Participation and Personal Development

Standard 8:   Partnership with Parents and Carers

Standard 9:   Multi-agency Working

Standard 10: The Community

Standard 11: Transition and Transfer

Standard 12: Professional Development

What is an audit?

An audit is defined as a transparent, systematic, objective evaluation, overview and quality assurance review process, which enables an educational setting to judge and compare its actual current Every Child Matters policy, practice, aims and values against a series of recommended predetermined best-practice ECM outcome evidence descriptors.

What are the benefits of undertaking the ECM Standards audit?

- ■ Quality auditing helps to compare what is with what is supposed to be happening within the educational setting in relation to ECM policy and practice.

- ■ An audit acts as a stocktaking self-review exercise on Every Child Matters, which is fundamental to identifying strengths and weaknesses and the ECM priorities for further development and improvement in the delivery of high-quality ECM outcomes.

- ■ Undertaking the audit for the ECM Standards will support and promote a shared sense of understanding and greater ownership among stakeholders for improving the Every Child Matters well-being outcomes for children and young people.

- ■ An audit will enable closer scrutiny of records, documentation and processes related to Every Child Matters that are maintained in the normal course of daily practice within the educational setting.

- ■ The audit serves intelligent accountability purposes in relation to Every Child Matters, i.e. the educational setting's own views of how well it is serving its client group of children and young people and setting its own priorities for improvement in ECM.

Four steps to carrying out the ECM Standards audit

1 *Initiation* – introducing the concept and process of the audit, explaining to stakeholders why it is necessary to undertake an audit for Every Child Matters.

2 *Planning* – how and when the ECM Standards audit will be undertaken, and who will be involved in the audit process.

3 *Implementation* – carrying out the ECM Standards audit, involving a range of participants.

4 *Reporting* – on the findings and outcome from the ECM Standards audit.

The ECM Standards audit report

On completion of the Every Child Matters Standards audit, a formal statement that summarises the results and main findings, in the form of an audit report, will help to inform the ECM Standards action plan.

The audit report must be clear and concise in disclosing all significant findings against each of the twelve ECM Standards, and suggest a systematic future improvement for Every Child Matters within the educational setting.

Both the completed initial audit and the audit report with the accompanying Every Child Matters Standards action plan must be included in the ECM portfolio of evidence.

An Every Child Matters Standards model action plan template is included at the end of this chapter. It is also available on the accompany CD as a Microsoft Word document, which enables it to be customised to suit the context of the educational setting.

Points to remember

The objective when undertaking the initial ECM Standards self-evaluation audit is to identify existing areas of strength in relation to Every Child Matters, as well as highlighting priorities for further development and improvement. The audit process entails:

■ completing the full initial audit to provide an overview of whether ECM policy and practice is emergent, developing or embedded against each of the Standards descriptors;

■ producing a report of findings that assists in informing the production of the ECM Standards action plan;

■ matching the twelve ECM Standards to the national and local priorities for development and improvement across a range of educational settings.

Standard 1: Ethos

EVERY CHILD MATTERS OUTCOME DESCRIPTORS	EMERGENT (early stages) ✓ or ✗	DEVELOPING (in progress) ✓ or ✗	EMBEDDED (fully in place) ✓ or ✗
BE HEALTHY			
An ethos of trust ensures children are free from bullying and discrimination			
The dietary needs of children from a diversity of ethnic groups or those who require special diets for medical reasons are respected and catered for			
Healthy eating and healthy lifestyles are promoted and encouraged among children, staff, parents			
Participation in physical exercise, sport and recreation is positively promoted			
An emotionally intelligent ethos enables children and staff to manage their feelings and emotions			
STAY SAFE			
Children and adults ensure that the safety of others and themselves is always a priority			
Risk assessments do not limit the opportunities for children to participate in outdoor activities, educational visits, residential holidays and foreign exchanges			
Children feel safe and secure in reporting bullying, discrimination and any incidents of dangerous behaviour			
ENJOY AND ACHIEVE			
An ethos of high expectations ensures that the full diversity of children achieve their optimum potential			
A positive ethos of a 'can do' approach to learning and well-being exists among children and staff			
Achievements however small are recognised and valued			
Children as active participants are empowered to take ownership for their learning and well-being			
The learning climate promotes experiential learning			
Children are proud to belong to the educational setting			

How to Achieve the Every Child Matters Standards, Paul Chapman Publishing © Rita Cheminais, 2007

EVERY CHILD MATTERS OUTCOME DESCRIPTORS	EMERGENT (early stages) ✓ or ✗	DEVELOPING (in progress) ✓ or ✗	EMBEDDED (fully in place) ✓ or ✗
MAKE A POSITIVE CONTRIBUTION			
An open ethos enables the views of children, parents/carers, staff and other partner/service providers to be valued, respected and acted upon			
An inclusive ethos fosters individual and collective responsibility in helping others			
Change is viewed as a positive development and children and staff are well supported in managing this			
A culture of community care, involvement and respect for the environment is promoted			
ACHIEVE ECONOMIC WELL-BEING			
The culture and ethos existing within the educational setting encourages enterprising activities and developments that enrich learning and well-being			
Children are encouraged to have realistic and optimistic aspirations, goals and expectations			
A welcoming ethos ensures that children and their parents/carers feel able to approach staff for advice and guidance to support their decision-making about future opportunities and life chances			
Team work and cooperative learning and social activities foster opportunities for children to take responsibility			

How to Achieve the Every Child Matters Standards, Paul Chapman Publishing © Rita Cheminais, 2007

Standard 2: Policy

EVERY CHILD MATTERS OUTCOME DESCRIPTORS	EMERGENT (early stages) ✓ or ✗	DEVELOPING (in progress) ✓ or ✗	EMBEDDED (fully in place) ✓ or ✗
BE HEALTHY			
There is a healthy eating policy in place which reflects the ECM outcome 'being healthy'			
There is a policy for PE and physical well-being, which emphasises the importance of regular exercise and physical fitness			
Policies for drugs and sex and relationships education reflect the ECM outcome 'being healthy', emphasising the importance of making appropriate lifestyle choices			
STAY SAFE			
The ECM outcome 'stay safe' is reflected in the Child Protection Policy and Safeguarding Children Policy			
The Health and Safety Policy reflects the ECM outcome 'stay safe', and children learn, play and socialise in a risk-free, accessible, safe environment			
The staffing policy makes explicit that all staff working with children are CRB checked			
The racial equality, anti-bullying and behaviour policies reflect the ECM outcome 'stay safe' and children are able to report any incidents of discrimination, harassment, bullying or anti-social behaviour			
ENJOY AND ACHIEVE			
The policies for curriculum, personalised learning, and teaching and learning reflect the ECM outcome 'enjoy and achieve', which is demonstrated in practice			
The policy on assessment for learning makes explicit the importance of tracking the progress of children and young people to prevent underachievement			
The assessment for learning policy ensures children and young people are involved in target-setting and reviewing their own progress in learning and well-being			

How to Achieve the Every Child Matters Standards, Paul Chapman Publishing © Rita Cheminais, 2007

⊙	EVERY CHILD MATTERS OUTCOME DESCRIPTORS	EMERGENT (early stages) ✓ or ✗	DEVELOPING (in progress) ✓ or ✗	EMBEDDED (fully in place) ✓ or ✗
MAKE A POSITIVE CONTRIBUTION	The PSHE and Citizenship policies reflect the ECM outcome 'make a positive contribution' and children and young people have a 'voice' and participate in decision-making			
	The Equal Opportunities and Inclusion Policies ensure that children and young people are able to contribute to out-of-hours learning activities and community			
	The Policy for Transition and Transfer to the next phase of education ensures that children and young people have a say and are consulted about their ECM provision, in the next educational setting			
ACHIEVE ECONOMIC WELL-BEING	Policies for work-related learning, 14–19, lifelong learning and/or business and enterprise ensure that children and young people develop economic awareness and become financially literate			

P   *How to Achieve the Every Child Matters Standards*, Paul Chapman Publishing © Rita Cheminais, 2007

Standard 3: The Environment

EVERY CHILD MATTERS OUTCOME DESCRIPTORS	EMERGENT (early stages) ✓ or ✗	DEVELOPING (in progress) ✓ or ✗	EMBEDDED (fully in place) ✓ or ✗
BE HEALTHY			
Calming music is utilised effectively within the setting to support the emotional well-being of children and staff			
Premises are kept clean and pleasant, and there are sufficient receptacles for litter within and outside the educational setting			
There is adequate ventilation, drinking water and healthy food options available at break and lunchtime			
The educational setting's outdoor environment offers sufficient space for play and physical exercise			
There is a quiet area within the setting available to children and staff to use for relaxation			
STAY SAFE			
Safety rules and hazard warnings are displayed in and around the educational setting and these are regularly referred to by children and staff			
The premises and surrounding grounds are well maintained, safe, secure and well lit			
Adaptations to premises enable access for wheelchair users and those with sensory impairments			
There is safe storage of equipment, medicines and any chemicals and cleaning products			
Staff are on duty at break and lunchtime to supervise the safety of children			

How to Achieve the Every Child Matters Standards, Paul Chapman Publishing © Rita Cheminais, 2007

	EVERY CHILD MATTERS OUTCOME DESCRIPTORS	EMERGENT (early stages) ✓ or ✗	DEVELOPING (in progress) ✓ or ✗	EMBEDDED (fully in place) ✓ or ✗
ENJOY AND ACHIEVE	The learning and recreational environment is welcoming, pleasant, interesting and stimulates enjoyable learning and play			
	There are attractive displays of children's work and achievements that celebrate and reflect the ECM outcome 'enjoy and achieve'			
	There are sufficient resources and facilities to enable children and adults to enjoy learning and achieve their optimum potential			
MAKE A POSITIVE CONTRIBUTION	The environment within the educational setting enables children and young people to feel confident in voicing their views and informing ECM decision-making in relation to improving their learning and recreational environment			
	Members of the local community are made welcome to enjoy the use of facilities and resources for learning and recreation as part of extended service provision, adult learning and/or family learning activities			
ACHIEVE ECONOMIC WELL-BEING	The educational setting's environment and facilities provide an appropriate venue for enterprising and income-generating activities to take place, which fund further learning opportunities or charitable organisations providing ECM well-being provision			
	The educational setting provides information and raises awareness about available local resources to support children and their families in relation to lifelong learning, training and employment opportunities			

Standard 4: Leadership and Management

EVERY CHILD MATTERS OUTCOME DESCRIPTORS	EMERGENT (early stages) ✓ or ✗	DEVELOPING (in progress) ✓ or ✗	EMBEDDED (fully in place) ✓ or ✗
BE HEALTHY			
The leader of the educational setting provides a positive role model to children and staff in relation to healthy eating, healthy lifestyles and emotional intelligence			
Distributed leadership ensures that staff share management responsibilities for ECM			
The work-life balance of children and staff is valued and respected			
STAY SAFE			
Leaders and managers for ECM policy and provision within the educational setting take safe risks, which do not compromise the learning and well-being of children and young people			
The safeguarding and protection of all children and young people within the educational setting is at the forefront of all ECM policy and service provision, and agreed procedures and guidelines are carried out by all staff			
ENJOY AND ACHIEVE			
There are clear ECM priorities and activities on the educational setting's development plan that are focused on improving the learning and well-being outcomes for children and young people			
The learning achievements of children, young people, staff, parents/carers and community members are celebrated and acknowledged			
High standards and challenging but realistic targets are set for children's learning, behaviour, attendance and ECM well-being outcomes			

How to Achieve the Every Child Matters Standards, Paul Chapman Publishing © Rita Cheminais, 2007

⊙	EVERY CHILD MATTERS OUTCOME DESCRIPTORS	EMERGENT (early stages) ✓ or ✗	DEVELOPING (in progress) ✓ or ✗	EMBEDDED (fully in place) ✓ or ✗
MAKE A POSITIVE CONTRIBUTION	All key stakeholders have been engaged in developing the ECM policy and provision to improve personalised learning and well-being			
	Stakeholders inform ECM decision-making through a range of discussion forums, focus groups, working parties and annual surveys			
	The contributions of stakeholders are highly valued and acknowledged in ECM review reports			
	The governing body/management board acts as a critical friend to the leadership team on ECM			
ACHIEVE ECONOMIC WELL-BEING	The leader of the educational setting takes the wider community view and seeks opportunities to engage local business and other service providers/educational settings in enterprising learning activities			

P *How to Achieve the Every Child Matters Standards*, Paul Chapman Publishing © Rita Cheminais, 2007

Standard 5: Personalised Learning

⊙	EVERY CHILD MATTERS OUTCOME DESCRIPTORS	EMERGENT (early stages) ✓ or ✗	DEVELOPING (in progress) ✓ or ✗	EMBEDDED (fully in place) ✓ or ✗
BE HEALTHY	An effective system of pastoral care exists to support the well-being and learning of children and young people			
	Children and young people are encouraged to feel good about themselves and are supported to develop their self-esteem, self-belief, self-image and personal worth			
	Children and young people are taught emotional intelligence to enable them to manage their own feelings and emotions, develop empathy and to understand and respect others' feelings			
STAY SAFE	Children and young people feel safe and secure to flourish as individuals within the educational setting			
	Children and young people know who to go to and where to seek further help when faced with potential danger, conflict or problems that create barriers to learning			
	Children and young people follow safety rules and procedures and behaviour codes of conduct during learning, recreational and social activities			
	Children and young people learn about safety awareness in the wider community, e.g. stranger danger, road safety			

How to Achieve the Every Child Matters Standards, Paul Chapman Publishing © Rita Cheminais, 2007

⊙	EVERY CHILD MATTERS OUTCOME DESCRIPTORS	EMERGENT (early stages) ✓ or ✗	DEVELOPING (in progress) ✓ or ✗	EMBEDDED (fully in place) ✓ or ✗
ENJOY AND ACHIEVE	Children and young people, as active participants in the personalised learning process, learn how to learn and acquire a repertoire of tools for learning			
	ICT and multimedia technology is exploited to enhance personalised learning tailored to meet individual needs			
	A range of teaching strategies and approaches is utilised to enhance personalised learning and creativity			
	Personalised learning builds on children and young people's prior knowledge, understanding, interests, strengths and aptitudes			
	Effective use of ECM data supports the planning of personalised learning and flexible learning pathways			
	Children and young people have opportunities to self-assess their learning and receive constructive feedback on what they need to do to further improve their learning and achievements			
MAKE A POSITIVE CONTRIBUTION	Children and young people have opportunities to contribute to the life and work of the educational setting			
	Children and young people's views are sought on the effectiveness of classroom learning experiences			
	Children and young people have a choice and a voice in the planning of personalised learning activities			
ACHIEVE ECONOMIC WELL-BEING	Children and young people are given appropriate impartial advice, guidance and support to make informed choices about their learning pathways and future goals			
	Children and young people are provided with out-of-hours learning for 'catch-up' and 'stretch' personalised learning activities			

P *How to Achieve the Every Child Matters Standards*, Paul Chapman Publishing © Rita Cheminais, 2007

Standard 6: Curriculum Entitlement, Access and Choice

	EVERY CHILD MATTERS OUTCOME DESCRIPTORS	EMERGENT (early stages) ✓ or ✗	DEVELOPING (in progress) ✓ or ✗	EMBEDDED (fully in place) ✓ or ✗
BE HEALTHY	Children and young people are taught about healthy eating and healthy lifestyles through a well planned Health Education curriculum programme			
STAY SAFE	The PSHE and Citizenship curriculum ensures children and young people are taught about personal safety, safety in society and the wider community			
ENJOY AND ACHIEVE	Children and young people have a choice in the personalised curriculum pathways they follow, tailored and customised to meet their individual needs			
	The whole curriculum is delivered using a range of accelerated learning approaches			
	Curriculum materials and resources reflect the ECM outcomes as well as portraying positive images of diversity			
	Access to the curriculum for a diversity of learners is enhanced by the use of ICT, technological aids and additional paraprofessional support where appropriate for removing barriers to learning, participation and well-being			
	Peer tutoring, coaching and mentoring are utilised to improve children and young people's access to the whole curriculum for learning and well-being			
	Curriculum planning takes account of the ECM outcomes and ensures equal opportunities for all			
	Opportunities for cross-curricular projects and initiatives related to the ECM outcomes are offered to children and young people			
	Distance flexible learning approaches are utilised when necessary to ensure curriculum continuity and progression for those children and young people unable to access their learning within the educational setting during prolonged periods of absence			
	Out-of-hours learning and recreational activities address the ECM outcomes			

How to Achieve the Every Child Matters Standards, Paul Chapman Publishing © Rita Cheminais, 2007

☺	EVERY CHILD MATTERS OUTCOME DESCRIPTORS	EMERGENT (early stages) ✓ or ✗	DEVELOPING (in progress) ✓ or ✗	EMBEDDED (fully in place) ✓ or ✗
MAKE A POSITIVE CONTRIBUTION	The PSHCE curriculum ensures children and young people develop the necessary social and personal development skills to make them more confident participants in the life and work of the educational setting			
	Children and young people have the opportunity to contribute their views about the curriculum which inform future planning, delivery, access and choice			
	Children and young people are offered impartial advice and guidance to enable them to make realistic and wise curriculum choices			
ACHIEVE ECONOMIC WELL-BEING	The curriculum enables children and young people to become lifelong learners and responsible citizens			
	The curriculum respects and responds to cultural diversity, environmental awareness and entrepreneurial activities			
	Partnerships beyond the educational setting promote community links and extend, enrich and enhance curriculum experiences for children and young people			

P *How to Achieve the Every Child Matters Standards*, Paul Chapman Publishing © Rita Cheminais, 2007

Standard 7: Presence, Participation and Personal Development

⊙	EVERY CHILD MATTERS OUTCOME DESCRIPTORS	EMERGENT (early stages) ✓ or ✗	DEVELOPING (in progress) ✓ or ✗	EMBEDDED (fully in place) ✓ or ✗
BE HEALTHY	Children and young people demonstrate tolerance, respect and empathy, and value difference and diversity			
	Children and young people are supported in developing emotionally and socially through the PSHCE curriculum			
STAY SAFE	Reasonable adjustments and fair treatment ensure that barriers to learning and participation are removed and minimised in order to provide a safe and secure ECM learning community			
	The educational setting has a well-established successful induction system to support new children, young people and staff joining the organisation			
ENJOY AND ACHIEVE	Children, young people, staff and adults enjoy opportunities to engage in cooperative and collaborative learning and social activities that enhance ECM outcomes			
	Children and young people develop positive attitudes to learning and well-being			
	Children and young people learn to respect and appreciate the achievements of other peers, no matter how small those achievements may be			
	A positive rewards system operates which acts as a good incentive to motivate children and young people to learn and achieve successful ECM outcomes			
	Children and young people have the opportunity to work independently, in pairs, as part of a group and as a whole class/cohort which promotes and develops social skills			

How to Achieve the Every Child Matters Standards, Paul Chapman Publishing © Rita Cheminais, 2007

EVERY CHILD MATTERS OUTCOME DESCRIPTORS	EMERGENT (early stages) ✓ or ✗	DEVELOPING (in progress) ✓ or ✗	EMBEDDED (fully in place) ✓ or ✗
MAKE A POSITIVE CONTRIBUTION			
Children, young people and staff are encouraged to adopt a solution-focused approach to resolving potential conflict or problems			
Children and young people contribute to democratic ECM decision-making via appropriate forums which focus on improving and enhancing presence, participation and personal development			
ACHIEVE ECONOMIC WELL-BEING			
Children and young people are provided with opportunities to take on leadership roles and to show initiative			
Children and young people are enabled to develop trust, understanding and the personal qualities to support them in coping with teenage and adult life			
Children and young people through team-building and team-work activities are able to relate successfully to other peers and adults			

How to Achieve the Every Child Matters Standards, Paul Chapman Publishing © Rita Cheminais, 2007

Standard 8: Partnership with Parents and Carers

EVERY CHILD MATTERS OUTCOME DESCRIPTORS	EMERGENT (early stages) ✓ or ✗	DEVELOPING (in progress) ✓ or ✗	EMBEDDED (fully in place) ✓ or ✗
BE HEALTHY			
Parents/carers are consulted about healthy eating options and the choice of food and drink available for their children within the educational setting			
Parents and carers are involved in supporting, promoting and modelling healthy lifestyles to their children			
Parents and carers are signposted to health and fitness activities locally, and are encouraged to participate in sport and physical fitness events			
Parents and carers have access to information and can attend workshop activities on how they can support the health and well-being of their children at home			
STAY SAFE			
Parents and carers have access to information related to child, home and family safety and security			
Parents and carers have the opportunity to participate in a range of workshops and classes related to aspects of safety, i.e. First Aid, Self-defence			
ENJOY AND ACHIEVE			
Parents and carers are encouraged to enrich and enhance the learning opportunities of children and young people within the educational setting and beyond			
The educational setting provides advice and strategies to enable parents and carers to support their children's learning, behaviour and well-being at home			
Parents and carers have the opportunity to participate in joint learning and well-being activities with their children, both within and beyond the educational setting			
Parents and carers are kept fully informed about the progress and achievements of their children in learning and ECM well-being outcomes			
The educational setting contacts parents and carers promptly to share good news as well as concerns about their child's learning, behaviour and well-being			

How to Achieve the Every Child Matters Standards, Paul Chapman Publishing © Rita Cheminais, 2007

EVERY CHILD MATTERS OUTCOME DESCRIPTORS	EMERGENT (early stages) ✓ or ✗	DEVELOPING (in progress) ✓ or ✗	EMBEDDED (fully in place) ✓ or ✗
MAKE A POSITIVE CONTRIBUTION			
Effective use is made of home/educational setting diaries to ensure two-way communication is maintained with parents and carers			
Active steps are taken to communicate with hard-to-reach parents/carers who have little or no contact with the educational setting			
The views of parents and carers are sought on ECM policy and practice, which are fed back, to inform decision-making in ECM provision to meet local needs			
Parents and carers have a point of contact for ECM in the educational setting, whom they can consult with			
Parents and carers receive advice and support on how to contribute to raising their children to become responsible citizens and lifelong learners			
ACHIEVE ECONOMIC WELL-BEING			
Parents and carers are made aware of the available local resources and how to access them in order to support lifelong learning			
Parents and carers' achievements and successes in relation to learning and well-being are acknowledged and celebrated within the educational setting sensitively			

Standard 9: Multi-agency Working

◯	EVERY CHILD MATTERS OUTCOME DESCRIPTORS	EMERGENT (early stages) ✓ or ✗	DEVELOPING (in progress) ✓ or ✗	EMBEDDED (fully in place) ✓ or ✗
BE HEALTHY	Frontline workers from multi-agency services provide advice, guidance and information to support the health and well-being of children and young people			
	Health service workers contribute to government health initiatives such as the Healthy Schools Award			
STAY SAFE	Professionals from education, health and social care fulfil their duties to safeguard, protect and promote the welfare of children and young people			
	Early intervention and preventative strategies are implemented by multi-agency service workers to ensure vulnerable children and young people do not develop unsafe lifestyles			
ENJOY AND ACHIEVE	Multi-agency service practitioners work in partnership with staff in the educational setting to remove barriers to learning and participation among children/young people			
	Multi-agency professionals provide valuable inputs to support the PSHE curriculum			
	Multi-agency staff, in partnership with key workers within the educational setting, track and monitor the behaviour and attendance of children and young people			
MAKE A POSITIVE CONTRIBUTION	The educational setting works closely with external multi-agency service providers, valuing the contributions they make to improving ECM outcomes for children			
	A collaborative 'Team Around the Child' approach to support and intervention contributes to coordinated effective, targeted, joined-up working to meet the needs of vulnerable children and young people			
	Joint professional development for ECM between multi-agency staff and staff within the education setting ensure common agreed targets focus on the impact of service provision on ECM outcomes			
	The views of multi-agency professionals working with children and young people in the setting are valued			

How to Achieve the Every Child Matters Standards, Paul Chapman Publishing © Rita Cheminais, 2007

⊙	EVERY CHILD MATTERS OUTCOME DESCRIPTORS	EMERGENT (early stages) ✓ or ✗	DEVELOPING (in progress) ✓ or ✗	EMBEDDED (fully in place) ✓ or ✗
MAKE A POSITIVE CONTRIBUTION	The impact of personalised services delivered by multi-agency partners is monitored and evaluated			
	Staff in the education setting know the external multi-agency services they can call on to improve ECM outcomes for vulnerable children			
	Children and young people are involved in the design and delivery of wraparound care and personalised services, which lead to better ECM outcomes			
ACHIEVE ECONOMIC WELL-BEING	Multi-agency service providers support children, young people and their families in maximising their economic and social well-being			
	Information and support is provided to children, young people and their families on welfare benefit entitlement			

P *How to Achieve the Every Child Matters Standards*, Paul Chapman Publishing © Rita Cheminais, 2007

Standard 10: The Community

EVERY CHILD MATTERS OUTCOME DESCRIPTORS	EMERGENT (early stages) ✓ or ✗	DEVELOPING (in progress) ✓ or ✗	EMBEDDED (fully in place) ✓ or ✗
BE HEALTHY			
A range of health and fitness information, workshops and activities is provided to members of the community which promote healthy lifestyles and healthy eating			
Refreshments and meals provided within the educational setting reflect cultural diversity within the local community			
Members of the community are consulted about health education programmes and health care provision offered at the educational setting to meet local needs			
STAY SAFE			
Safety in the community is promoted among children and young people through the PSHE and Citizenship programmes			
Community links with local services, i.e. St John Ambulance, fire service, police, are maximised to inform children and young people about safety at home, and beyond			
Signposting to further support and information regarding safety from harm, domestic violence and crime in the community is available to children, young people and families			
ENJOY AND ACHIEVE			
The richness and diversity of the community is utilised as a valuable resource to extend learning opportunities for children and young people			
Children and young people have the opportunity to enjoy joint learning and recreational activities with members from the local community			
Out-of-hours learning and recreational opportunities and facilities are provided within and near the educational setting, for members and groups of the local community			
Children and young people experience a range of community-based learning activities which involve them in joint initiatives and projects with other educational settings			

⊙	EVERY CHILD MATTERS OUTCOME DESCRIPTORS	EMERGENT (early stages) ✓ or ✗	DEVELOPING (in progress) ✓ or ✗	EMBEDDED (fully in place) ✓ or ✗
MAKE A POSITIVE CONTRIBUTION	Children and young people have the opportunity to contribute to and participate in a range of community activities which involve volunteering, fundraising and community care, including local, national and global environmental projects			
	Members of the community are engaged in decision-making about ECM provision to meet local needs			
	Children and young people, through their involvement with the community, develop skills and knowledge about responsible citizenship			
ACHIEVE ECONOMIC WELL-BEING	Community figures and local businesses are invited into the educational setting in order to impart and share their experiences of economic enterprises and/or support learning and well-being initiatives through sponsorship			
	Opportunities are sought for children and young people to engage in supervised and organised enterprising activities in partnership with local businesses			
	Any income generated or profits made from community charges for using and accessing facilities and out-of-hours learning and recreational activities is ploughed back into the educational setting's budget to fund future learning and well-being activities			

Standard 11: Transition and Transfer

(o) EVERY CHILD MATTERS OUTCOME DESCRIPTORS	EMERGENT (early stages) ✓ or ✗	DEVELOPING (in progress) ✓ or ✗	EMBEDDED (fully in place) ✓ or ✗
BE HEALTHY Children and young people are prepared emotionally, well in advance, for transfer to the next phase of education			
A peer buddy and mentoring system exists which supports the well-being of children and young people during transfer and transition			
Parents and carers are provided with information, guidance and advice about how to support the emotional well-being of their child during and throughout key transition and transfer periods			
Advice, guidance and support is offered to children and their parents/carers about healthy eating options available in the next educational setting			
STAY SAFE Joint collaborative planning for transition and transfer between staff ensures that children and young people feel safe and secure, and look forward to the next year, key stage or phase of education			
ENJOY AND ACHIEVE Taster sessions, induction and open-day transfer events provide children and young people with a range of activities and experiences in the next phase of education			
Children and young people enjoy a sample of learning and ECM well-being activities in preparation for transition to the next year group or key stage within the same educational setting			
Effective ECM data analysis and information sharing help to inform appropriate grouping, setting and teaching and pastoral support arrangements for the next year, key stage or phase of education			
Transition and transfer planning ensure continuity in personalised learning and personalised services to meet ECM well-being outcomes for children and young people			

P *How to Achieve the Every Child Matters Standards*, Paul Chapman Publishing © Rita Cheminais, 2007

(o) EVERY CHILD MATTERS OUTCOME DESCRIPTORS	EMERGENT (early stages) ✓ or ✗	DEVELOPING (in progress) ✓ or ✗	EMBEDDED (fully in place) ✓ or ✗
MAKE A POSITIVE CONTRIBUTION			
Parents and carers' views and involvement in relation to transition and transfer of their child are actively sought, and these inform future planning and decision-making			
Children and young people have the opportunity to express their views and experiences about transition and transfer to inform future decision-making			
Staff involved in supporting transition and transfer contribute their views and experiences, which helps to inform future CPD in this aspect			
Staff between educational settings and year groups have the opportunity to network and disseminate best practice in transition and transfer			
ACHIEVE ECONOMIC WELL-BEING			
Transfer visits to the next educational setting help children and young people to consider their future personalised learning and lifelong learning pathways			
The educational setting's transition and transfer policy clearly reflects how children and young people are supported to achieve economic and social well-being during these key periods of time			
Children and young people are able to build on their personal experiences and knowledge from the previous year, key stage or phase of education			

P *How to Achieve the Every Child Matters Standards, Paul Chapman Publishing © Rita Cheminais, 2007*

Standard 12: Professional Development

○	EVERY CHILD MATTERS OUTCOME DESCRIPTORS	EMERGENT (early stages) ✓ or ✗	DEVELOPING (in progress) ✓ or ✗	EMBEDDED (fully in place) ✓ or ✗
BE HEALTHY	Staff well-being within the educational setting is high-focus in order to enable them to have quality time to undertake relevant ECM professional development while maintaining a healthy work/life balance			
	Staff workload, induction and training commitments are realistic and manageable, and do not compromise the well-being of children and young people			
STAY SAFE	Staff participate in relevant ongoing training related to child protection and safeguarding children			
	All staff, adults and volunteers working with children and young people within the educational setting are CRB checked			
	Staff have engaged in emotional intelligence professional development, which enables children and young people to feel safe in sharing their emotions and feelings in the presence of trusting adults/peers			
ENJOY AND ACHIEVE	Staff enjoy networking and collaborating on ECM with their colleagues and those in other educational settings to improve outcomes for children			
	Staff gain personal reward in knowing that their ECM professional development has had a positive impact on improving the learning and well-being of children			
	Staff benefit from and enjoy engaging in utilising coaching and mentoring strategies to move ECM practice forward within the educational setting			
	Staff build up portfolios of professional development which acknowledge their achievements and impact on improving ECM and personalised learning outcomes for children and young people			

	EVERY CHILD MATTERS OUTCOME DESCRIPTORS	EMERGENT (early stages) ✓ or ✗	DEVELOPING (in progress) ✓ or ✗	EMBEDDED (fully in place) ✓ or ✗
MAKE A POSITIVE CONTRIBUTION	The ECM strengths, talents, expertise, skills and knowledge of staff within the educational setting are maximised in order to make effective positive contributions to improving ECM outcomes for children			
	Staff have the opportunity to contribute to ECM consultation and feed back their views to inform programmes of professional development for ECM			
	Team work and collaboration at all levels contribute to developing ECM staff leadership and management			
	The staff fully understand the relationship between performance management, CPD and sustained improvement in contributing to the learning and ECM well-being outcomes for children and young people			
ACHIEVE ECONOMIC WELL-BEING	Staff are empowered to be creative and innovative in seeking opportunities to engage children and young people in worthwhile enterprising activities			
	Staff CPD related to ECM leads to new and exciting future professional opportunities and potential promotion within the educational setting, EIP and across local networks, clusters and federations			

How to Achieve the Every Child Matters Standards, Paul Chapman Publishing © Rita Cheminais, 2007

Every Child Matters Standards Action Plan 200 _ to 200 _

ECM Standard	Action/activities	Lead person(s) responsible	Resources	Timesale (from/to)	Monitoring (who, when, how)	Success criteria (impact/outcomes)
1. Ethos						
2. Policy						
3. The Environment						
4. Leadership and Management						
5. Personalised Learning						
6. Curriculum Entitlement, access and choice						
7. Presence, participation and personal development						
8. Partnership with Parents and Carers						
9. Multi-agency Working						
10. The Community						
11. Transition and Transfer						
12. Professional development						

How to Achieve the Every Child Matters Standards, Paul Chapman Publishing © Rita Cheminais, 2007

Building an Every Child Matters portfolio of evidence

This chapter provides an in-depth guide to establishing an Every Child Matters Standards portfolio of evidence for submission as part of the final assessment process towards achieving the ECM Standard Award. It describes:

- the benefits and purpose of utilising the portfolio of evidence approach;

- the stages in building a portfolio of evidence for the ECM Standards;

- the types and format of evidence to collect and include in the portfolio;

- how to use and complete the twelve ECM Standards portfolio checklists.

Introduction

A portfolio is an organised collection of a range of quality information and evidence on policy and practice related to achieving the Every Child Matters outcomes, to present for assessment. It acts as a showcase of your best achievements and experiences in this aspect of development. The portfolio as a dynamic evidence base, tells the story of the journey you have travelled in order to reach the desired outcomes.

Building an Every Child Matters (ECM) portfolio of evidence is a crucial part of informing the planning and development of ECM provision within the educational setting. It will involve the ongoing collection of relevant and telling evidence that demonstrates the impact of ECM policy, activities and provision in working towards achieving the Every Child Matters Standards.

When compiling an Every Child Matters portfolio of evidence it is important to respond to a number of searching self-evaluation prompts in order to enable the educational setting to explore and reflect on its ECM policy and practice in greater depth.

Purpose and benefits of a portfolio

The portfolio approach, as part of the self-evaluation process, is a valuable way of enabling educational settings to gather evidence in order to judge their progress in relation to successfully meeting and improving the five Every Child Matters outcomes for children and young people.

Compiling a portfolio of Every Child Matters outcomes evidence, aligned with the twelve ECM Standards, is also an ideal means of contributing to meeting the Ofsted inspection requirements. It also informs other stakeholders such as the local authority, the School Improvement Partner (SIP) and the governing body or management board about the achievements in this aspect, within the educational setting, in the local community or cluster group.

In a nutshell, the advantages of compiling an ECM portfolio of evidence are:

- to identify strengths and areas for further improvement in ECM;

- to disseminate examples of good practice in ECM;

- to involve a range of stakeholders in contributing to, and participating in, the evidence-gathering process.

Stages in building a portfolio of evidence

- *Stage 1*. Respond to the checklist of reflective prompts for considering the range and quality of the educational settings evidence, to meet each ECM Standard.

- *Stage 2*. Refer to the range of the examples offered to inform the nature of the evidence you can gather and submit for each ECM Standard.

- *Stage 3*. Record and include the evidence you have for your current and planned ECM policy, practice and provision within the portfolio, and signpost or cross-reference where further sources of evidence can be located for each ECM Standard.

Portfolio checklist

- The contents of the portfolio provide a clear, well-organised navigation structure.

- The significant evidence material adds value to the portfolio.

- The format of the evidence is easily understood.

- Supporting evidence is in the preferred format, i.e. documents, digital web-based and/or CD-ROM computer-based, are clearly identifiable against the relevant standards.

- The portfolio is an accurate representation of progress made.

What to include in the ECM portfolio of evidence

The ECM portfolio will only be as good as the quality and reliability of the range of ongoing telling evidence collected to meet each Every Child Matters Standard. The forms and types of evidence to gather for the portfolio are as follows.

Observation

This type of evidence will be undertaken by a 'critical friend' and/or an external assessor who will observe ECM outcome activities and provision first hand, as well as viewing digital and photographic evidence, capturing children's and young people's ECM outcome achievements.

Oral Evidence

This type of evidence, available from a wide range of participants/stakeholders, can be recorded via audio tape, video, CD-ROM/DVD, website, ECM chat room forums, e-mails.

Written evidence

The written evidence will include:

- Every Child Matters Policy for the educational setting;

- school profile, prospectus, information brochures/leaflets for the setting;

- the educational setting's mission statement which reflects ECM outcomes;

- improvement plan/development plan for the setting indicating ECM priority(s);

- data – evidence and analysis of progress towards meeting ECM outcomes;

- the completed and updated Ofsted self-evaluation form (SEF) for the educational setting;

- snapshots of good and outstanding ECM practice taken from the most recent Ofsted inspection report;

- other relevant external ECM monitoring and evaluation reports;

- individual significant case studies – cameos of 'real stories' of successful ECM outcomes;

- relevant minutes of significant meetings focusing on ECM developments, e.g. from the ECM focus group, working party, or the change team;

- reports and digital/CD-ROM evidence from ECM showcase activities, projects or initiatives;

- media accounts, promotional information, newsletters related to ECM in the educational setting;

- feedback from stakeholder surveys, questionnaires, interviews, letters, e-mails;

- snapshots of evidence from children and young people's ECM logs and diaries, records of achievement, progress files and written work demonstrating ECM outcomes;

- statements and testimonials from other partner organisations and services.

Collecting evidence for the Every Child Matters Standards

On the following pages you will find the information and resources required to compile a portfolio of evidence, towards meeting the ECM Standards. Each page focuses on one of the twelve ECM Standards, which includes:

- the initial ECM Standard statement;

- a checklist of prompts to support the sourcing of evidence;

- examples of the type of evidence to collect for the Standard;

- evidence collected with signposting and cross-referencing to further sources of evidence.

Each of these twelve pages should be included in the final portfolio of evidence, with the accompanying relevant evidence sources.

These pages are available on the accompanying CD and can be downloaded from the relevant Microsoft Word document file.

Points to remember

Building a portfolio of evidence for the ECM Standards to present for final external assessment is part of regular ongoing self-evaluation. The ECM Standards portfolio of evidence:

- enables a good range of evidence to be gathered in different formats from various stakeholders;

- provides an accurate representation of progress made towards fully achieving each ECM Standard;

- contributes a valuable range of evidence for the Ofsted self-evaluation form (SEF) and the School Improvement Partner (SIP);

- supports the dissemination of good practice in Every Child Matters.

Standard 1: Ethos

Everyone – every child/young person and every adult – matters in the educational setting, where the ethos promotes positive attitudes and awareness of the needs of the whole child/young person or individual.

Ethos checklist

- Our vision and mission statement for Every Child Matters is clear and displayed.

- Our educational setting is welcoming, friendly and safe.

- The staff are emotionally intelligent.

- Children/young people and the staff are proud to belong to this educational setting.

- The views and positive contributions of children/young people and their parents/carers are respected and valued.

- The learning and well-being of everyone in this educational setting matters.

- A high level of openness and trust exists within the educational setting.

Evidence

Examples of the type of evidence to collect: mission statement; prospectus; information leaflets and brochures; ECM policy; newsletters; website; displays; school profile; snapshots of the child's/young person's 'voice' and the views of parents/carers, governors, staff, members of the community and external partners/service providers; staff INSET on ECM

Evidence collected	Cross-reference/signpost to further sources of evidence
•	
•	
•	
•	
•	
•	
•	
•	
•	

Standard 2: Policy

The Every Child Matters well-being outcomes are reflected in all policies within the educational setting and are promoted in everyday practice.

Policy checklist

- All policies in the educational setting reflect a commitment to Every Child Matters.

- The Every Child Matters policy is evident in everyday practice within the educational setting.

- The aims and principles of the Every Child Matters policy are well publicised and are displayed in the reception area.

- Everyone who works with and supports the learning and well-being of our children and young people, on- and off-site, is familiar with and understands the educational setting's Every Child Matters Policy.

Evidence

Examples of the type of evidence to collect: ECM policy for the educational setting; reports on monitoring and evaluating ECM policy; extracts and samples from other key policies; ECM policy summaries for parents/carers; school profile; prospectus; information leaflets and brochures on ECM; feedback from stakeholder surveys and questionnaires; records of involvement of stakeholders in ECM policy development; minutes from significant meetings such as those of the ECM focus group/working party; the educational setting's website

Evidence collected	Cross-reference/signpost to further sources of evidence
•	
•	
•	
•	
•	
•	
•	
•	
•	
•	

Standard 3: The Environment

The environment within the educational setting is safe and healthy; it promotes enjoyment in learning; it values individual contributions and secures personal and social well-being and economic awareness

Environment checklist

- The physical environment within the educational setting is well maintained, pleasant and risk-free.

- There is a peace zone or quiet place available within the setting for children/young people and adults to utilise.

- Children and young people thrive in the setting's environment, which promotes and meets the Every Child Matters well-being outcomes.

- Children and young people are able to take safe risks in their learning, within an environment that promotes experiential learning.

- Displays in learning areas and along corridors of children's and young people's work show clear links to the ECM outcomes.

Evidence

Examples of the type of evidence to collect: displays of children and young people's work and achievements; celebratory assemblies; presentation and awards ceremonies; picture gallery on the setting website; prospectus; ECM five outcomes on display in and around the setting; clean, bright, safe and well-ventilated learning and play areas

Evidence collected	Cross-reference/signpost to further sources of evidence
•	
•	
•	
•	
•	
•	
•	
•	
•	
•	

Standard 4: Leadership and Management

The leadership and management of the Every Child Matters change for children strategy provides a clear direction, distributed empowerment, ownership and accountability for implementing and achieving the five Every Child Matters outcomes.

Leadership and Management checklist

- The leader and head of the educational setting promotes a clear shared vision for Every Child Matters with all stakeholders.

- All staff and other key stakeholders have been actively engaged in developing the ECM vision, policy and provision.

- Members of the senior leadership team play a key role in managing, monitoring and evaluating ECM provision and outcomes.

- The development/improvement plan features priorities and activities to support the implementation and achievement of the ECM outcomes.

- An ECM focus group/change team oversees the ongoing development and progress of Every Child Matters.

- The head of the setting keeps the governing body/management committee or board up to date regarding progress made towards achieving the ECM outcomes.

- Governors and staff from within the educational setting, which includes those staff supporting children/young people from external services, undertake relevant professional development related to Every Child Matters.

Evidence

Examples of the type of evidence to collect: ECM policy; mission statement/vision statement for ECM; development/improvement plan ECM priorities; minutes of significant meetings related to ECM; prospectus; information leaflets for parents/carers on ECM; job descriptions for all staff leading and managing ECM outcomes; evaluation feedback from stakeholder surveys and questionnaires on leadership and management of ECM; records of attendance and impact of ECM INSET for governors, staff, parents/carers and children/young people; Ofsted report

Evidence collected	Cross-reference/signpost to further sources of evidence
•	
•	
•	
•	
•	
•	
•	
•	
•	
•	

Standard 5: Personalised Learning

Personalised learning, which builds on children and young people's interests, aptitudes and strengths, making education more responsive to individual learners' needs, promotes high expectations, enjoyment and appropriate challenges in learning, within and beyond the educational setting.

Personalised Learning checklist

- Children and young people are active participants in the personalised learning process.

- Children and young people assess and review their own personalised provision and progress towards successfully meeting the ECM outcomes.

- Children and young people can follow flexible, tailored, appropriate, personalised curriculum pathways.

- Flexible timetabling and grouping arrangements promote personalisation to support and meet children and young people's learning and well-being needs.

- Productive partnerships with parents/carers, external service providers and members of the local community promote and develop lifelong learning opportunities and effective citizenship among children and young people within the educational setting.

- ICT and multimedia technology are utilised effectively to develop and support personalised learning.

Evidence

Examples of the type of evidence to collect: evidence from direct observation of teaching and learning and out-of-hours learning activities; curriculum policy and provision; policies for teaching and learning, assessment for learning, ECM policy; feedback from surveys and views of stakeholders (children/young people, parents/carers, external partners/service providers) on personalised learning

Evidence collected	Cross-reference/signpost to further sources of evidence
•	
•	
•	
•	
•	
•	
•	
•	
•	
•	

Standard 6: Curriculum Entitlement, Access and Choice

The planning, organisation and delivery of the whole curriculum for learning and well-being, which includes out-of-hours learning opportunities, reflect the Every Child Matters outcomes, ensuring equality of opportunity, choice and access for the full diversity of children and young people.

Curriculum checklist

- Every child/young person has an entitlement to access a broad, relevant, interesting and personalised curriculum which enables them to reach their optimum potential.

- The curriculum is delivered utilising a range of accelerated learning approaches, including coaching, mentoring and modelling, which enthuse and inspire learning.

- The curriculum promotes and encourages children and young people to become lifelong learners and responsible citizens.

- Materials and learning resources across the curriculum reflect and promote the Every Child Matters outcomes.

- The curriculum responds to cultural diversity, environmental awareness and entrepreneurial activity.

- The educational setting maximises the community's potential as a resource to enhance and enrich curriculum opportunities for learning and well-being.

Evidence

Examples of the type of evidence to collect: curriculum policy and provision outline; samples of curriculum planning, monitoring and evaluation reports; PSHE and Citizenship curriculum plans, policy and provision; careers policy and provision; information about transition and transfer for curriculum continuity and progression in relation to ECM outcomes; destinations of learners post-16; evidence of cross-curricular projects and initiatives for ECM; examples of extended services and out-of-hours learning opportunities supporting ECM outcomes

Evidence collected	Cross-reference/signpost to further sources of evidence
•	
•	
•	
•	
•	
•	
•	
•	
•	
•	
•	

How to Achieve the Every Child Matters Standards, Paul Chapman Publishing © Rita Cheminais, 2007

Standard 7: Presence, Participation and Personal Development

A diversity of children and young people are represented in the educational setting, who demonstrate tolerance, respect and responsibility; they participate in a range of activities, developing into confident, healthy, self-managing lifelong learners and citizens.

Presence, Participation and Personal Development checklist

- A solution-focused approach to identify barriers to learning and participation is adopted which ensures fair treatment and reasonable adjustments are made.

- A good induction system exists which provides peer support and mentoring for new children, young people and staff joining the educational setting.

- Children, young people and staff are able to express their opinions and views in making positive contributions to informing decision-making.

- Children, young people and staff are emotionally intelligent, demonstrating empathy and understanding in valuing difference and diversity.

- Children and young people are empowered to resolve conflict and tension to improve their well-being.

- Children, young people and adults enjoy opportunities to participate in cooperative and collaborative learning and social activities during and beyond the school day.

Evidence

Examples of the type of evidence to collect: policies for ECM – Inclusion, behaviour, SEN, Equal Opportunities, Accessibility; PSHE and Citizenship programmes of study; induction programme for new pupils and staff; job descriptions for PSHE coordinator, learning mentor, pupil counsellors, family support workers; meeting minutes from school/pupil councils or forums; evaluation from out-of-hours learning activities; data analysis of attendance, exclusions; sampling records of achievement, progress files

Evidence collected	Cross-reference/signpost to further sources of evidence
•	
•	
•	
•	
•	
•	
•	
•	
•	
•	

Standard 8: Partnership with Parents and Carers

The educational setting works proactively in partnership with parents and carers to enable them to support their child's learning and Every Child Matters well-being outcomes.

Parent Partnership checklist

- Workshops and classes for parents/carers offer practical strategies, guidance and advice on supporting their child in achieving the Every Child Matters outcomes.

- Parents/carers are kept informed about their child's progress in the ECM outcomes.

- Family learning opportunities help to engage children and their parents/carers together in enjoyable learning and healthy lifestyle activities.

- There is an active parent group and support network that enables parents/carers to inform ECM provision within the educational setting.

- There is a first point of contact in the educational setting to respond to any queries from parents/carers related to Every Child Matters.

- Parents/carers are made aware of the setting's Every Child Matters policy.

Evidence

Examples of the type of evidence to collect: prospectus; information leaflets for parents; feedback from parents/carers surveys; minutes of meetings from parents' group; website for parents; letters and e-mails from parents/carers; newsletters; facilities for parents/carers within the educational setting

Evidence collected	Cross-reference/signpost to further sources of evidence
•	
•	
•	
•	
•	
•	
•	
•	
•	
•	

Standard 9: Multi-agency Working

The educational setting works in partnership with external multi-agency service providers to meet the agreed Every Child Matters objectives and targets in order to improve outcomes for children and young people.

Multi-agency Working checklist

- There is a senior member of staff who commissions, coordinates and oversees multi-agency provision delivered within the education setting.

- The educational setting ensures, through the lead professional, that they contribute to the Common Assessment Framework (CAF) process.

- The educational setting makes prompt referrals to external multi-agency services.

- The roles and responsibilities of frontline workers from multi-agency services supporting children/young people within the setting are made explicit.

- The impact of external multi-agency service provision in improving the ECM outcomes for children/young people is routinely monitored and evaluated.

Evidence

Examples of the type of evidence to collect: service level agreements; multi-agency information leaflets; relevant service provider/setting websites; minutes of meetings with multi-agency service providers; job descriptions of those delivering and coordinating ECM services; feedback from multi-agency surveys/questionnaires; joint setting staff/service INSET feedback

Evidence collected	Cross-reference/signpost to further sources of evidence
•	
•	
•	
•	
•	
•	
•	
•	
•	
•	

Standard 10: The Community

The involvement and participation of the community in the Every Child Matters programme of change for children builds cohesion while ensuring that everyone matters in the local learning community.

Community checklist

■ The community has the opportunity to contribute to improving personalised learning and ECM well-being outcomes for children and young people.

■ The community provides a valuable resource to promote and support Every Child Matters developments within the educational setting.

■ The needs of the community influence and inform the ECM provision within the educational setting.

■ The educational setting takes the wider view, seeking new partners from the community to deliver services to enhance Every Child Matters provision.

■ Open and trusting relationships exist between the educational setting and the community.

■ The educational setting acts as an ECM 'hub' for the community to engage in a range of educational, social, leisure, cultural and entrepreneurial activities to improve outcomes for children, young people and their families.

Evidence

Examples of the type of evidence to collect: programme of community activities; minutes of community group meetings; community priority on development/improvement plan; policy statement for community engagement; customer care policy; feedback from community surveys/questionnaires; testimonial statements from the community about ECM provision/activities; audit and evaluation report outlining response to community needs; newsletters; prospectus

Evidence collected	Cross-reference/signpost to further sources of evidence
•	
•	
•	
•	
•	
•	
•	
•	
•	
•	

Standard 11: Transition and Transfer

The educational setting has effective transition and transfer procedures to promote continuity and progression in relation to children and young people achieving the Every Child Matters well-being outcomes.

Transition and Transfer checklist

- There is a clear transition and transfer policy which outlines the arrangements for a seamless managed move for ECM.

- Children and young people are consulted and fully involved in the development of transition and transfer ECM support programmes.

- There is an ECM peer buddy system operating to support the induction of new children/young people joining the setting at any point during the year.

- Information-sharing and CAF procedures between service providers, ensure continuity in personalised learning and ECM well-being provision, cross-phase.

- Open days and taster personalised learning and ECM well-being sessions are available to help children/young people feel secure and look forward to transition and transfer.

- An ECM transition and transfer programme of support is available to parents/carers as part of family learning and extended service provision.

Evidence

Examples of the type of evidence to collect: transition and transfer policy; transition and transfer induction programme for stakeholders; evaluation and statement of stakeholder transition and transfer experiences; buddy system overview; prospectus; displays, CD/DVD, website link related to ECM transition and transfer; sample of transition plans for children/young people.

Evidence collected	Cross-reference/signpost to further sources of evidence
•	
•	
•	
•	
•	
•	
•	
•	
•	
•	

Standard 12: Professional Development

The educational setting promotes a continuous professional development programme for Every Child Matters, which supports capacity building to equip a skilled and knowledge-able learning and well-being workforce to meet the needs of children and young people.

ECM Professional Development checklist

- There is an induction programme for new staff which covers Every Child Matters and identifies future training needs in this aspect.

- Training on Every Child Matters for staff, governors, parents/carers and children/young people is linked to the relevant ECM priorities on the development plan.

- Work shadowing, coaching and mentoring are utilised as part of the staff professional development programme to develop skills and expertise in ECM.

- The impact of ECM staff training is evidenced through appraisal and the performance management review process.

- Staff build a professional development portfolio of evidence which reflects ECM training and records staff contributions to improve ECM outcomes for children.

- Networking with other educational settings/services promotes the exchange of staff expertise, ideas and best practice in ECM.

Evidence

Examples of the type of evidence to collect: CPD programme; INSET evaluations; sampling portfolios of professional development; CPD policy; pupil evaluations of lessons and personalised services; job description of the leader of CPD; snapshots/cameos of staff CPD reviews on impact of ECM training; overview of staffing qualifications and posts, i.e. AST, Excellent Teachers, HLTAs with ECM responsibilities

Evidence collected	Cross-reference/signpost to further sources of evidence
•	
•	
•	
•	
•	
•	
•	
•	
•	
•	
•	

HAPTER 5

The Every Child Matters evidence descriptors for the twelve Standards

This chapter revisits and provides the entire Every Child Matters Standards framework. It emphasises the importance of educational settings recording their evidence in full at embedded level, matched against each descriptor within each of the twelve Standards. Most importantly, the chapter confirms:

■ the relevance of utilising the Every Child Matters Standards across a range of different educational settings in order to address and improve national priorities, such as personalisation, transition, pupil voice;

■ the twelve Every Child Matters Standards statements;

■ the telling evidence required to confirm each ECM Standard descriptor has been met at embedded level;

■ the recording of the impact, where appropriate, in improving the ECM outcomes for pupils.

Introduction

The Every Child Matters government strategy is one of the most far-reaching radical programmes of change aimed at improving the lives of children, young people and their families. Educational settings as universal service providers play a crucial role in ensuring that the learning and well-being of every child and young person matters.

The twelve Every Child Matters Standards with their outcome evidence descriptors enable any educational setting catering for children and young people from three to 19, to have a clear and consistent baseline from which to make valid judgements about their progress towards meeting the Every Child Matters outcomes.

The Every Child Matters Standards cover twelve aspects which are relevant across a range of different educational settings and phases of education. The twelve ECM Standards outcome descriptors can be tailored and customised to suit the particular age range of children and young people in the setting, for example personalised for early years or post-16, without altering the focus of the descriptors. The twelve ECM Standards descriptors take into account the national context and agenda within which educational settings in the twenty-first century are operating.

For example, the government's expectation is that every school will become an extended school. Personalisation, providing personalised services and tailored education, will ensure that every child and young person, regardless of their background, reaches their optimum potential and experiences improved life chances. Increased engagement with the community to extend and enhance lifelong learning opportunities will ensure that members of the community play a greater part in informing extended and personalised service provision within their local area.

Improving transition and transfer for children and young people, which can be a traumatic experience for some children who are vulnerable or who have learning difficulties and disabilities, will ensure greater continuity in learning and progression. Engaging children and young people, as active participants, to have a greater voice and choice will ensure that personalised services, personalised learning and flexible curriculum pathways meet individual needs. Improving joined-up coordinated, multi-agency partnership working will ensure that a more efficient Children's Workforce is able to deliver effective universal, targeted and specialist services in and around educational settings. Strengthening partnership with parents and carers, will ensure that their contributions in supporting their child's learning and well-being are valued.

The twelve Every Child Matters Standards

- *Standard 1: Ethos*. Everyone – every child/young person and every adult – matters in the educational setting, where the ethos promotes positive attitudes and awareness of the needs of the whole child/young person or individual.

- *Standard 2: Policy*. The Every Child Matters well-being outcomes are reflected in all policies within the educational setting and are promoted in everyday practice.

- *Standard 3: The Environment*. The environment within the educational setting is safe and healthy; it promotes enjoyment in learning; it values individual contributions and secures personal and social well-being and economic awareness.

- *Standard 4: Leadership and Management*. The leadership and management of the Every Child Matters Change for Children strategy provide a clear direction, distributed empowerment, ownership and accountability for implementing and achieving the Every Child Matters five outcomes.

- *Standard 5: Personalised Learning.* Personalised learning, which builds on children and young people's interests, aptitudes and strengths, making education more responsive to individual learners' needs, promotes high expectations, enjoyment and appropriate challenges in learning, within and beyond the educational setting.

- *Standard 6: Curriculum Entitlement, Access and Choice.* The planning, organisation and delivery of the whole curriculum for learning and well-being, which includes out-of-hours learning opportunities, reflect the Every Child Matters outcomes, ensuring equality of opportunity, choice and access for the full diversity of children and young people.

- *Standard 7: Presence, Participation and Personal Development.* A diversity of children and young people are represented in the educational setting who demonstrate tolerance, respect and responsibility; they participate in a range of activities, developing into confident, healthy, self-managing lifelong learners and citizens.

- *Standard 8: Partnership with Parents and Carers.* The educational setting works proactively in partnership with parents and carers to enable them to support their child's learning and Every Child Matters well-being outcomes.

- *Standard 9: Multi-agency Working.* The educational setting works in partnership with external multi-agency service providers to meet the agreed Every Child Matters objectives and targets, in order to improve outcomes for children and young people.

- *Standard 10: The Community.* The involvement and participation of the community in the Every Child Matters programme of change for children and young people builds cohesion, while ensuring that everyone matters in the local learning community.

- *Standard 11: Transition and Transfer.* The educational setting has effective transition and transfer procedures to promote continuity and progression in relation to children and young people achieving the Every Child Matters well-being outcomes.

- *Standard 12: Professional Development.* The educational setting promotes a continuous professional development programme for Every Child Matters, which supports capacity building to equip a skilled and knowledgeable learning and well-being workforce to meet the needs of children and young people.

Using the Every Child Matters Standards

Each Every Child Matters Standard is underpinned by a series of outcome descriptors, aligned with the Every Child Matters five outcomes for children and young people. For any individual educational setting to achieve the Every Child Matters Standards Award, they have to fulfil each descriptor in every one of the twelve standards at the embedded level. Those educational settings forming part of a cluster group, federation, EIP or networked learning community will each have to achieve ECM Standards 1 and 2 at embedded level, while the other ten ECM Standards can be achieved at embedded level collectively between and across all the settings. The eventual goal will be for each individual educational setting within the group to achieve their own ECM Standards Award as opposed to obtaining a shared cluster award, having each met all the twelve ECM Standards at embedded level.

There is nothing to prevent an educational setting adding further descriptors to each Every Child Matters Standard. However, this will not influence any final decision in relation to achieving the Every Child Matters Standards Award, which will be judged on the specified given descriptors in each Standard.

There is an expectation that each of the twelve completed Every Child Matters Standards evidence tables, with accompanying evidence, will be included in the final portfolio of evidence.

Individual educational settings and clusters of settings can undertake their own moderation of the Every Child Matters Standards and outcomes, which will provide a local benchmark to support final judgements. This is a helpful process to undertake, but it is not compulsory, as external assessors will ensure that their moderation supports valid judgements from individual and clusters of educational settings participating in the award scheme.

Each of the twelve Every Child Matters Standards evidence tables is available on the accompanying CD as a Microsoft Word document. This will enable those in educational settings responsible for collecting evidence for the ECM portfolio to complete and save electronically the ECM Standard information they have gathered against each evidence descriptor.

Points to remember

- The ECM Standards are appropriate to and transferable across a range of different educational settings.

- They respond to other competing educational priorities as well as the ECM agenda, i.e. personalised learning, transition, partnerships, community engagement.

- The twelve ECM Standards statements and evidence descriptors provide a benchmark for evaluating and judging the progress made towards achieving each Standard at embedded level.

EVERY CHILD MATTERS STANDARDS EVIDENCE TABLES

Standard 1: Ethos

(o)	EVERY CHILD MATTERS OUTCOME DESCRIPTORS	EMERGENT (early stages) ✓ or ✗	DEVELOPING (in progress) ✓ or ✗	EMBEDDED (fully in place) ✓ or ✗	EVALUATIVE COMMENTS/ EVIDENCE AND IMPACT ON PUPILS' OUTCOMES (WHERE APPROPRIATE)
BE HEALTHY	An ethos of trust ensures children are free from bullying and discrimination				
	The dietary needs of children from a diversity of ethnic groups or those who require special diets for medical reasons are respected and catered for				
	Healthy eating and healthy lifestyles are promoted and encouraged among children, staff, parents				
	Participation in physical exercise, sport and recreation is positively promoted				
	An emotionally intelligent ethos enables children and staff to manage their feelings and emotions				
STAY SAFE	Children and adults ensure that the safety of others and themselves is always a priority				
	Risk assessments do not limit the opportunities for children to participate in outdoor activities, educational visits, residential holidays and foreign exchanges				
	Children feel safe and secure in reporting bullying, discrimination and any incidents of dangerous behaviour				
ENJOY AND ACHIEVE	An ethos of high expectations ensures that the full diversity of children achieve their optimum potential				
	A positive ethos of a 'can do' approach to learning and well-being exists among children and staff				
	Achievements however small are recognised and valued				
	Children as active participants are empowered to take ownership for their learning and well-being				
	The learning climate promotes experiential learning				
	Children are proud to belong to the educational setting				

How to Achieve the Every Child Matters Standards, Paul Chapman Publishing © Rita Cheminais, 2007

EVERY CHILD MATTERS OUTCOME DESCRIPTORS	EMERGENT (early stages) ✓ or ✗	DEVELOPING (in progress) ✓ or ✗	EMBEDDED (fully in place) ✓ or ✗	EVALUATIVE COMMENTS/ EVIDENCE AND IMPACT ON PUPILS' OUTCOMES (WHERE APPROPRIATE)
MAKE A POSITIVE CONTRIBUTION An open ethos enables the views of children, parents/carers, staff and other partner/service providers to be valued, respected and acted upon				
An inclusive ethos fosters individual and collective responsibility in helping others				
Change is viewed as a positive development and children and staff are well supported in managing this				
A culture of community care, involvement and respect for the environment is promoted				
ACHIEVE ECONOMIC WELL-BEING The culture and ethos existing within the educational setting encourages enterprising activities and developments that enrich learning and well-being				
Children are encouraged to have realistic and optimistic aspirations, goals and expectations				
A welcoming ethos ensures that children and their parents/carers feel able to approach staff for advice and guidance to support their decision-making about future opportunities and life chances				
Team work and cooperative learning and social activities foster opportunities for children to take responsibility				

P *How to Achieve the Every Child Matters Standards*, Paul Chapman Publishing © Rita Cheminais, 2007

Standard 2: Policy

	EVERY CHILD MATTERS OUTCOME DESCRIPTORS	EMERGENT (early stages) ✓ or ✗	DEVELOPING (in progress) ✓ or ✗	EMBEDDED (fully in place) ✓ or ✗	EVALUATIVE COMMENTS/ EVIDENCE AND IMPACT ON PUPILS' OUTCOMES (WHERE APPROPRIATE)
BE HEALTHY	There is a healthy eating policy in place which reflects the ECM outcome 'being healthy'				
	There is a policy for PE and physical well-being, which emphasises the importance of regular exercise and physical fitness				
	Policies for drugs and sex and relationships education reflect the ECM outcome 'being healthy', emphasising the importance of making appropriate lifestyle choices				
STAY SAFE	The ECM outcome 'stay safe' is reflected in the Child Protection Policy and Safeguarding Children Policy				
	The Health and Safety Policy reflects the ECM outcome 'stay safe', and children learn, play and socialise in a risk-free, accessible, safe environment				
	The staffing policy makes explicit that all staff working with children are CRB checked				
	The racial equality, anti-bullying and behaviour policies reflect the ECM outcome 'stay safe' and children are able to report any incidents of discrimination, harassment, bullying or anti-social behaviour				
ENJOY AND ACHIEVE	The policies for curriculum, personalised learning, and teaching and learning reflect the ECM outcome 'enjoy and achieve', which is demonstrated in practice				
	The policy on assessment for learning makes explicit the importance of tracking the progress of children and young people to prevent underachievement				
	The assessment for learning policy ensures children and young people are involved in target-setting and reviewing their own progress in learning and well-being				

P *How to Achieve the Every Child Matters Standards*, Paul Chapman Publishing © Rita Cheminais, 2007

⊙	EVERY CHILD MATTERS OUTCOME DESCRIPTORS	EMERGENT (early stages) ✓ or ✗	DEVELOPING (in progress) ✓ or ✗	EMBEDDED (fully in place) ✓ or ✗	EVALUATIVE COMMENTS/ EVIDENCE AND IMPACT ON PUPILS' OUTCOMES (WHERE APPROPRIATE)
MAKE A POSITIVE CONTRIBUTION	The PSHE and Citizenship policies reflect the ECM outcome 'make a positive contribution' and children and young people have a 'voice' and participate in decision-making				
	The Equal Opportunities and Inclusion Policies ensure that children and young people are able to contribute to out-of-hours learning activities and community projects				
	The Policy for Transition and Transfer to the next phase of education ensures that children and young people have a say and are consulted about their ECM provision in the next educational setting				
ACHIEVE ECONOMIC WELL-BEING	Policies for work-related learning, 14–19, lifelong learning and/or business and enterprise ensure that children and young people develop economic awareness and become financially literate				

P *How to Achieve the Every Child Matters Standards*, Paul Chapman Publishing © Rita Cheminais, 2007

Standard 3: The Environment

	EVERY CHILD MATTERS OUTCOME DESCRIPTORS	EMERGENT (early stages) ✓ or ✗	DEVELOPING (in progress) ✓ or ✗	EMBEDDED (fully in place) ✓ or ✗	EVALUATIVE COMMENTS/ EVIDENCE AND IMPACT ON PUPILS' OUTCOMES (WHERE APPROPRIATE)
BE HEALTHY	Calming music is utilised effectively within the setting to support the emotional well-being of children and staff				
	Premises are kept clean and pleasant, and there are sufficient receptacles for litter within and outside the educational setting				
	There is adequate ventilation, drinking water and healthy food options available at break and lunchtime				
	The educational setting's outdoor environment offers sufficient space for play and physical exercise				
	There is a quiet area within the setting available to children and staff to use for relaxation				
STAY SAFE	Safety rules and hazard warnings are displayed in and around the educational setting and these are regularly referred to by children and staff				
	The premises and surrounding grounds are well maintained, safe, secure and well lit				
	Adaptations to premises enable access for wheelchair users and those with sensory impairments				
	There is safe storage of equipment, medicines and any chemicals and cleaning products				
	Staff are on duty at break and lunchtime to supervise the safety of children				
ENJOY AND ACHIEVE	The learning and recreational environment is welcoming, pleasant, interesting and stimulates enjoyable learning and play				
	There are attractive displays of children's work and achievements that celebrate and reflect the ECM outcome 'enjoy and achieve'				
	There are sufficient resources and facilities to enable children and adults to enjoy learning and achieve their optimum potential				

How to Achieve the Every Child Matters Standards, Paul Chapman Publishing © Rita Cheminais, 2007

	EVERY CHILD MATTERS OUTCOME DESCRIPTORS	EMERGENT (early stages) ✓ or X	DEVELOPING (in progress) ✓ or X	EMBEDDED (fully in place) ✓ or X	EVALUATIVE COMMENTS/ EVIDENCE AND IMPACT ON PUPILS' OUTCOMES (WHERE APPROPRIATE)
MAKE A POSITIVE CONTRIBUTION	The environment within the educational setting enables children and young people to feel confident in voicing their views and informing ECM decision-making in relation to improving their learning and recreational environment				
	Members of the local community are made welcome to enjoy the use of facilities and resources for learning and recreation as part of extended service provision, adult learning and/or family learning activities				
ACHIEVE ECONOMIC WELL-BEING	The educational setting's environment and facilities provide an appropriate venue for enterprising and income-generating activities to take place, which fund further learning opportunities or charitable organisations providing ECM well-being provision				
	The educational setting provides information and raises awareness about available local resources to support children and their families in relation to lifelong learning, training and employment opportunities				

Standard 4: Leadership and Management

	EVERY CHILD MATTERS OUTCOME DESCRIPTORS	EMERGENT (early stages) ✓ or ✗	DEVELOPING (in progress) ✓ or ✗	EMBEDDED (fully in place) ✓ or ✗	EVALUATIVE COMMENTS/ EVIDENCE AND IMPACT ON PUPILS' OUTCOMES (WHERE APPROPRIATE)
BE HEALTHY	The leader of the educational setting provides a positive role model to children and staff in relation to healthy eating, healthy lifestyles and emotional intelligence				
	Distributed leadership ensures that staff share management responsibilities for ECM				
	The work/life balance of children and staff is valued and respected				
STAY SAFE	Leaders and managers for ECM policy and provision within the educational setting take safe risks which do not compromise the learning and well-being of children and young people				
	The safeguarding and protection of all children and young people within the educational setting is at the forefront of all ECM policy and service provision, and agreed procedures and guidelines are carried out by all staff				
ENJOY AND ACHIEVE	There are clear ECM priorities and activities on the educational setting's development plan that are focused on improving the learning and well-being outcomes for children and young people				
	The learning achievements of children, young people, staff, parents/carers and community members are celebrated and acknowledged				
	High standards and challenging but realistic targets are set for children's learning, behaviour, attendance and ECM well-being outcomes				

How to Achieve the Every Child Matters Standards, Paul Chapman Publishing © Rita Cheminais, 2007

⊙	EVERY CHILD MATTERS OUTCOME DESCRIPTORS	EMERGENT (early stages) ✓ or ✗	DEVELOPING (in progress) ✓ or ✗	EMBEDDED (fully in place) ✓ or ✗	EVALUATIVE COMMENTS/ EVIDENCE AND IMPACT ON PUPILS' OUTCOMES (WHERE APPROPRIATE)
MAKE A POSITIVE CONTRIBUTION	All key stakeholders have been engaged in developing the ECM policy and provision to improve personalised learning and well-being				
	Stakeholders inform ECM decision-making through a range of discussion forums, focus groups, working parties and annual surveys				
	The contributions of stakeholders are highly valued and acknowledged in ECM review reports				
	The governing body/management board acts as a critical friend to the leadership team on ECM				
ACHIEVE ECONOMIC WELL-BEING	The leader of the educational setting takes the wider community view and seeks opportunities to engage local business and other service providers/educational settings in enterprising learning activities				

P   *How to Achieve the Every Child Matters Standards*, Paul Chapman Publishing © Rita Cheminais, 2007

Standard 5: Personalised Learning

	EVERY CHILD MATTERS OUTCOME DESCRIPTORS	EMERGENT (early stages) ✓ or ✗	DEVELOPING (in progress) ✓ or ✗	EMBEDDED (fully in place) ✓ or ✗	EVALUATIVE COMMENTS/ EVIDENCE AND IMPACT ON PUPILS' OUTCOMES (WHERE APPROPRIATE)
BE HEALTHY	An effective system of pastoral care exists to support the well-being and learning of children and young people				
	Children and young people are encouraged to feel good about themselves and are supported to develop their self-esteem, self-belief, self-image and personal worth				
	Children and young people are taught emotional intelligence to enable them to manage their own feelings and emotions, develop empathy and to understand and respect others' feelings				
STAY SAFE	Children and young people feel safe and secure to flourish as individuals within the educational setting				
	Children and young people know who to go to and where to seek further help when faced with potential danger, conflict or problems that create barriers to learning				
	Children and young people follow safety rules and procedures and behaviour codes of conduct during learning, recreational and social activities				
	Children and young people learn about safety awareness in the wider community, e.g. stranger danger, road safety				
ENJOY AND ACHIEVE	Children and young people, as active participants in the personalised learning process, learn how to learn and acquire a repertoire of tools for learning				
	ICT and multimedia technology is exploited to enhance personalised learning tailored to meet individual needs				
	A range of teaching strategies and approaches is utilised to enhance personalised learning and creativity				
	Personalised learning builds on children and young people's prior knowledge, understanding, interests, strengths and aptitudes				
	Effective use of ECM data supports the planning of personalised learning and flexible learning pathways				
	Children and young people have opportunities to self-assess their own learning and receive constructive feedback on what they need to do to further improve their learning and achievements				

How to Achieve the Every Child Matters Standards, Paul Chapman Publishing © Rita Cheminais, 2007

	EVERY CHILD MATTERS OUTCOME DESCRIPTORS	EMERGENT (early stages) ✓ or ✗	DEVELOPING (in progress) ✓ or ✗	EMBEDDED (fully in place) ✓ or ✗	EVALUATIVE COMMENTS/ EVIDENCE AND IMPACT ON PUPILS' OUTCOMES (WHERE APPROPRIATE)
MAKE A POSITIVE CONTRIBUTION	Children and young people have opportunities to contribute to the life and work of the educational setting				
	Children and young people's views are sought on the effectiveness of classroom learning experiences				
	Children and young people have a choice and a voice in the planning of personalised learning activities				
ACHIEVE ECONOMIC WELL-BEING	Children and young people are given appropriate impartial advice, guidance and support to make informed choices about their learning pathways and future goals				
	Children and young people are provided with out-of-hours learning for 'catch-up' and 'stretch' personalised learning activities				

How to Achieve the Every Child Matters Standards, Paul Chapman Publishing © Rita Cheminais, 2007

Standard 6: Curriculum Entitlement, Access and Choice

	EVERY CHILD MATTERS OUTCOME DESCRIPTORS	EMERGENT (early stages) ✓ or ✗	DEVELOPING (in progress) ✓ or ✗	EMBEDDED (fully in place) ✓ or ✗	EVALUATIVE COMMENTS/ EVIDENCE AND IMPACT ON PUPILS' OUTCOMES (WHERE APPROPRIATE)
BE HEALTHY	Children and young people are taught about healthy eating and healthy lifestyles through a well-planned Health Education curriculum programme				
STAY SAFE	The PSHE and Citizenship curriculum ensures children and young people are taught about personal safety, safety in society and the wider community				
ENJOY AND ACHIEVE	Children and young people have a choice in the personalised curriculum pathways they follow, tailored and customised to meet their individual needs				
	The whole curriculum is delivered using a range of accelerated learning approaches				
	Curriculum materials and resources reflect the ECM outcomes as well as portraying positive images of diversity				
	Access to the curriculum for a diversity of learners is enhanced by the use of ICT, technological aids and additional paraprofessional support where appropriate for removing barriers to learning, participation and well-being				
	Peer tutoring, coaching and mentoring are utilised to improve children and young people's access to the whole curriculum for learning and well-being				
	Curriculum planning takes account of the ECM outcomes and ensures equal opportunities for all				
	Opportunities for cross-curricular projects and initiatives related to the ECM outcomes are offered to children and young people				
	Distance flexible learning approaches are utilised when necessary to ensure curriculum continuity and progression for those children and young people unable to access their learning within the educational setting during prolonged periods of absence				
	Out-of-hours learning and recreational activities address the ECM outcomes				

How to Achieve the Every Child Matters Standards, Paul Chapman Publishing © Rita Cheminais, 2007

	EVERY CHILD MATTERS OUTCOME DESCRIPTORS	EMERGENT (early stages) ✓ or ✗	DEVELOPING (in progress) ✓ or ✗	EMBEDDED (fully in place) ✓ or ✗	EVALUATIVE COMMENTS/ EVIDENCE AND IMPACT ON PUPILS' OUTCOMES (WHERE APPROPRIATE)
MAKE A POSITIVE CONTRIBUTION	The PSHCE curriculum ensures children and young people develop the necessary social and personal development skills to make them more confident participants in the life and work of the educational setting				
	Children and young people have the opportunity to contribute their views about the curriculum which inform future planning, delivery, access and choice				
	Children and young people are offered impartial advice and guidance to enable them to make realistic and wise curriculum choices				
ACHIEVE ECONOMIC WELL-BEING	The curriculum enables children and young people to become lifelong learners and responsible citizens				
	The curriculum respects and responds to cultural diversity, environmental awareness and entrepreneurial activities				
	Partnerships beyond the educational setting promote community links and extend, enrich and enhance curriculum experiences for children and young people				

P *How to Achieve the Every Child Matters Standards*, Paul Chapman Publishing © Rita Cheminais, 2007

Standard 7: Presence, Participation and Personal Development

	EVERY CHILD MATTERS OUTCOME DESCRIPTORS	EMERGENT (early stages) ✓ or ✗	DEVELOPING (in progress) ✓ or ✗	EMBEDDED (fully in place) ✓ or ✗	EVALUATIVE COMMENTS/ EVIDENCE AND IMPACT ON PUPILS' OUTCOMES (WHERE APPROPRIATE)
BE HEALTHY	Children and young people demonstrate tolerance, respect and empathy and value difference and diversity				
	Children and young people are supported in developing emotionally and socially through the PSHCE curriculum				
STAY SAFE	Reasonable adjustments and fair treatment ensure that barriers to learning and participation are removed and minimised in order to provide a safe and secure ECM learning community				
	The educational setting has a well established successful induction system to support new children, young people and staff joining the organisation				
ENJOY AND ACHIEVE	Children, young people, staff and adults enjoy opportunities to engage in cooperative and collaborative learning and social activities that enhance ECM outcomes				
	Children and young people develop positive attitudes to learning and well-being				
	Children and young people learn to respect and appreciate the achievements of other peers, no matter how small those achievements may be				
	A positive rewards system operates which acts as a good incentive to motivate children and young people to learn and achieve successful ECM outcomes				
	Children and young people have the opportunity to work independently, in pairs, as part of a group and as a whole class/cohort which promotes and develops social skills				

P   *How to Achieve the Every Child Matters Standards*, Paul Chapman Publishing © Rita Cheminais, 2007

⊙	EVERY CHILD MATTERS OUTCOME DESCRIPTORS	EMERGENT (early stages) ✓ or ✗	DEVELOPING (in progress) ✓ or ✗	EMBEDDED (fully in place) ✓ or ✗	EVALUATIVE COMMENTS/ EVIDENCE AND IMPACT ON PUPILS' OUTCOMES (WHERE APPROPRIATE)
MAKE A POSITIVE CONTRIBUTION	Children, young people and staff are encouraged to adopt a solution-focused approach to resolving potential conflict or problems				
	Children and young people contribute to democratic ECM decision-making via appropriate forums which focus on improving and enhancing presence, participation and personal development				
ACHIEVE ECONOMIC WELL-BEING	Children and young people are provided with opportunities to take on leadership roles and to show initiative				
	Children and young people are enabled to develop trust, understanding and the personal qualities to support them in coping with teenage and adult life				
	Children and young people through team-building and team-work activities are able to relate successfully to other peers and adults				

P *How to Achieve the Every Child Matters Standards*, Paul Chapman Publishing © Rita Cheminais, 2007

Standard 8: Partnership with Parents and Carers

	EVERY CHILD MATTERS OUTCOME DESCRIPTORS	EMERGENT (early stages) ✓ or ✗	DEVELOPING (in progress) ✓ or ✗	EMBEDDED (fully in place) ✓ or ✗	EVALUATIVE COMMENTS/EVIDENCE AND IMPACT ON PUPILS' OUTCOMES (WHERE APPROPRIATE)
BE HEALTHY	Parents/carers are consulted about healthy eating options and the choice of food and drink available for their children within the educational setting				
	Parents and carers are involved in supporting, promoting and modelling healthy lifestyles to their children				
	Parents and carers are signposted to health and fitness activities locally, and are encouraged to participate in sport and physical fitness events				
	Parents and carers have access to information and can attend workshop activities on how they can support the health and well-being of their children at home				
STAY SAFE	Parents and carers have access to information related to child, home and family safety and security				
	Parents and carers have the opportunity to participate in a range of workshops and classes related to aspects of safety, i.e. first aid, self-defence				
ENJOY AND ACHIEVE	Parents and carers are encouraged to enrich and enhance the learning opportunities of children and young people within the educational setting and beyond				
	The educational setting provides advice and strategies to enable parents and carers to support their children's learning, behaviour and well-being at home				
	Parents and carers have the opportunity to participate in joint learning and well-being activities with their children, both within and beyond the educational setting				
	Parents and carers are kept fully informed about the progress and achievements of their children in learning and ECM well-being outcomes				
	The educational setting contacts parents and carers promptly to share good news as well as concerns about their child's learning, behaviour and well-being				

P   *How to Achieve the Every Child Matters Standards*, Paul Chapman Publishing © Rita Cheminais, 2007

	EVERY CHILD MATTERS OUTCOME DESCRIPTORS	EMERGENT (early stages) ✓ or ✗	DEVELOPING (in progress) ✓ or ✗	EMBEDDED (fully in place) ✓ or ✗	EVALUATIVE COMMENTS/ EVIDENCE AND IMPACT ON PUPILS' OUTCOMES (WHERE APPROPRIATE)
MAKE A POSITIVE CONTRIBUTION	Effective use is made of home/educational setting diaries to ensure two-way communication is maintained with parents and carers				
	Active steps are taken to communicate with hard-to-reach parents/carers who have little or no contact with the educational setting				
	The views of parents and carers are sought on ECM policy and practice, which are fed back, to inform decision-making in ECM provision to meet local needs				
	Parents and carers have a point of contact for ECM in the educational setting, whom they can consult with				
	Parents and carers receive advice and support on how to contribute to raising their children to become responsible citizens and lifelong learners				
ACHIEVE ECONOMIC WELL-BEING	Parents and carers are made aware of the available local resources and how to access them in order to support lifelong learning				
	Parents' and carers' achievements and successes in relation to learning and well-being are acknowledged and celebrated within the educational setting sensitively				

How to Achieve the Every Child Matters Standards, Paul Chapman Publishing © Rita Cheminais, 2007

Standard 9: Multi-agency Working

	EVERY CHILD MATTERS OUTCOME DESCRIPTORS	EMERGENT (early stages) ✓ or ✗	DEVELOPING (in progress) ✓ or ✗	EMBEDDED (fully in place) ✓ or ✗	EVALUATIVE COMMENTS/ EVIDENCE AND IMPACT ON PUPILS' OUTCOMES (WHERE APPROPRIATE)
BE HEALTHY	Frontline workers from multi-agency services provide advice, guidance and information to support the health and well-being of children and young people				
	Health service workers contribute to government health initiatives such as the Healthy Schools Award				
STAY SAFE	Professionals from education, health and social care fulfil their duties to safeguard, protect and promote the welfare of children and young people				
	Early intervention and preventative strategies are implemented by multi-agency service workers to ensure vulnerable children and young people do not develop unsafe lifestyles				
ENJOY AND ACHIEVE	Multi-agency service practitioners work in partnership with staff in the educational setting to remove barriers to learning and participation among children/young people				
	Multi-agency professionals provide valuable inputs to support the PSHE curriculum				
	Multi-agency staff, in partnership with key workers within the educational setting, track and monitor the behaviour and attendance of children and young people				
	Lead professionals from multi-agency services coordinate the CAF process and liaise with staff within the educational setting to ensure better ECM outcomes for children and young people				

How to Achieve the Every Child Matters Standards, Paul Chapman Publishing © Rita Cheminais, 2007

EVERY CHILD MATTERS OUTCOME DESCRIPTORS	EMERGENT (early stages) ✓ or ✗	DEVELOPING (in progress) ✓ or ✗	EMBEDDED (fully in place) ✓ or ✗	EVALUATIVE COMMENTS/ EVIDENCE AND IMPACT ON PUPILS' OUTCOMES (WHERE APPROPRIATE)
MAKE A POSITIVE CONTRIBUTION				
The educational setting works closely with external multi-agency service providers, valuing the contributions they make to improving ECM outcomes for children				
A collaborative 'Team Around the Child' approach to support and intervention contributes to coordinated, effective, targeted, joined-up working to meet the needs of vulnerable children and young people				
Joint professional development for ECM between multi-agency staff and staff within the education setting ensure that common agreed targets focus on the impact of service provision on ECM outcomes				
The views of multi-agency professionals working with children and young people in the setting are valued				
The impact of personalised services delivered by multi-agency partners is monitored and evaluated				
Staff in the education setting know the external multi-agency services they can call on to improve ECM outcomes for vulnerable children				
Children and young people are involved in the design and delivery of wraparound care and personalised services, which lead to better ECM outcomes				
ACHIEVE ECONOMIC WELL-BEING Multi-agency service providers support children, young people and their families in maximising their economic and social well-being				
Information and support is provided to children, young people and their families on welfare benefit entitlement				

How to Achieve the Every Child Matters Standards, Paul Chapman Publishing © Rita Cheminais, 2007

Standard 10: The Community

	EVERY CHILD MATTERS OUTCOME DESCRIPTORS	EMERGENT (early stages) ✓ or ✗	DEVELOPING (in progress) ✓ or ✗	EMBEDDED (fully in place) ✓ or ✗	EVALUATIVE COMMENTS/ EVIDENCE AND IMPACT ON PUPILS' OUTCOMES (WHERE APPROPRIATE)
BE HEALTHY	A range of health and fitness information, workshops and activities is provided to members of the community which promote healthy lifestyles and healthy eating				
	Refreshments and meals provided within the educational setting reflect cultural diversity within the local community				
	Members of the community are consulted about health education programmes and health care provision offered at the educational setting to meet local needs				
STAY SAFE	Safety in the community is promoted among children and young people through the PSHE and Citizenship programmes				
	Community links with local services, i.e. St John Ambulance, fire service, police, are maximised to inform children and young people about safety at home and beyond				
	Signposting to further support and information regarding safety from harm, domestic violence and crime in the community is available to children, young people and families				
ENJOY AND ACHIEVE	The richness and diversity of the community is utilised as a valuable resource to extend learning opportunities for children and young people				
	Children and young people have the opportunity to enjoy joint learning and recreational activities with members from the local community				
	Out-of-hours learning and recreational opportunities and facilities are provided within and near the educational setting for members and groups of the local community				
	Children and young people experience a range of community-based learning activities which involve them in joint initiatives and projects with other educational settings				

How to Achieve the Every Child Matters Standards, Paul Chapman Publishing © Rita Cheminais, 2007

EVERY CHILD MATTERS OUTCOME DESCRIPTORS	EMERGENT (early stages) ✓ or X	DEVELOPING (in progress) ✓ or X	EMBEDDED (fully in place) ✓ or X	EVALUATIVE COMMENTS/ EVIDENCE AND IMPACT ON PUPILS' OUTCOMES (WHERE APPROPRIATE)
MAKE A POSITIVE CONTRIBUTION				
Children and young people have the opportunity to contribute to and participate in a range of community activities which involve volunteering, fundraising and, community care, including local, national and global environmental projects				
Members of the community are engaged in decision-making about ECM provision to meet local needs				
Children and young people, through their involvement with the community, develop skills and knowledge about responsible citizenship				
ACHIEVE ECONOMIC WELL-BEING				
Community figures and local businesses are invited into the educational setting in order to impart and share their experiences of economic enterprises and/or support learning and well-being initiatives through sponsorship				
Opportunities are sought for children and young people to engage in supervised and organised enterprising activities in partnership with local businesses				
Any income generated or profits made from community charges for using and accessing facilities and out-of-hours learning and recreational activities is ploughed back into the educational setting's budget to fund future learning and well-being activities				

How to Achieve the Every Child Matters Standards, Paul Chapman Publishing © Rita Cheminais, 2007

Standard 11: Transition and Transfer

EVERY CHILD MATTERS OUTCOME DESCRIPTORS	EMERGENT (early stages) ✓ or ✗	DEVELOPING (in progress) ✓ or ✗	EMBEDDED (fully in place) ✓ or ✗	EVALUATIVE COMMENTS/ EVIDENCE AND IMPACT ON PUPILS' OUTCOMES (WHERE APPROPRIATE)
BE HEALTHY Children and young people are prepared emotionally, well in advance, for transfer to the next phase of education				
A peer buddy and mentoring system exists which supports the well-being of children and young people during transfer and transition				
Parents and carers are provided with information, guidance and advice about how to support the emotional well-being of their child during and throughout key transition and transfer periods				
Advice, guidance and support is offered to children and their parents/carers about healthy eating options available in the next educational setting				
STAY SAFE Joint collaborative planning for transition and transfer between staff ensures that children and young people feel safe and secure, and look forward to the next year, key stage or phase of education				
ENJOY AND ACHIEVE Taster sessions, induction and open-day transfer events provide children and young people with a range of activities and experiences in the next phase of education				
Children and young people enjoy a sample of learning and ECM well-being activities in preparation for transition to the next year group or key stage within the same educational setting				
Effective ECM data analysis and information sharing helps to inform appropriate grouping, setting and teaching and pastoral support arrangements for the next year, key stage or phase of education				
Transition and transfer planning ensures continuity in personalised learning and personalised services to meet ECM well-being outcomes for children and young people				

How to Achieve the Every Child Matters Standards, Paul Chapman Publishing © Rita Cheminais, 2007

EVERY CHILD MATTERS OUTCOME DESCRIPTORS	EMERGENT (early stages) ✓ or ✗	DEVELOPING (in progress) ✓ or ✗	EMBEDDED (fully in place) ✓ or ✗	EVALUATIVE COMMENTS/ EVIDENCE AND IMPACT ON PUPILS' OUTCOMES (WHERE APPROPRIATE)
MAKE A POSITIVE CONTRIBUTION Parents' and carers' views and involvement in relation to transition and transfer of their child are actively sought, and these inform future planning and decision-making				
Children and young people have the opportunity to express their views and experiences about transition and transfer to inform future decision-making				
Staff involved in supporting transition and transfer contribute their views and experiences, which helps to inform future CPD in this aspect				
Staff between educational settings and year groups have the opportunity to network and disseminate best practice in transition and transfer				
ACHIEVE ECONOMIC WELL-BEING Transfer visits to the next educational setting help children and young people to consider their future personalised learning and lifelong learning pathways				
The educational settings transition and transfer policy clearly reflects how children and young people are supported to achieve economic and social well-being during these key periods of time				
Children and young people are able to build on their personal experiences and knowledge from the previous year, key stage or phase of education				

Standard 12: Professional Development

	EVERY CHILD MATTERS OUTCOME DESCRIPTORS	EMERGENT (early stages) ✓ or ✗	DEVELOPING (in progress) ✓ or ✗	EMBEDDED (fully in place) ✓ or ✗	EVALUATIVE COMMENTS/ EVIDENCE AND IMPACT ON PUPILS' OUTCOMES (WHERE APPROPRIATE)
BE HEALTHY	Staff well-being within the educational setting is high-focus in order to enable them to have quality time to undertake relevant ECM professional development while maintaining a healthy work/life balance				
	Staff workload, induction and training commitments are realistic and manageable, and do not compromise the well-being of children and young people				
STAY SAFE	Staff participate in relevant ongoing training related to child protection and safe-guarding children				
	All staff, adults and volunteers working with children and young people within the educational setting are CRB checked				
	Staff have engaged in emotional intelligence professional development, which enables children and young people to feel safe in sharing their emotions and feelings in the presence of trusting adults/peers				
ENJOY AND ACHIEVE	Staff enjoy networking and collaborating on ECM with their colleagues and those in other educational settings to improve outcomes for children				
	Staff gain personal reward in knowing that their ECM professional development has had a positive impact on improving the learning and well-being of children				
	Staff benefit from and enjoy engaging in utilising coaching and mentoring strategies to move ECM practice forward within the educational setting				
	Staff build up portfolios of professional development which acknowledge their achievements and impact on improving ECM and personalised learning outcomes for children and young people				

How to Achieve the Every Child Matters Standards, Paul Chapman Publishing © Rita Cheminais, 2007

EVERY CHILD MATTERS OUTCOME DESCRIPTORS	EMERGENT (early stages) ✓ or ✗	DEVELOPING (in progress) ✓ or ✗	EMBEDDED (fully in place) ✓ or ✗	EVALUATIVE COMMENTS/ EVIDENCE AND IMPACT ON PUPILS' OUTCOMES (WHERE APPROPRIATE)
MAKE A POSITIVE CONTRIBUTION				
The ECM strengths, talents, expertise, skills and knowledge of staff within the educational setting are maximised in order to make effective positive contributions to improving ECM outcomes for children				
Staff have the opportunity to contribute to ECM consultation and feed back their views to inform programmes of professional development for ECM				
Teamwork and collaboration at all levels contribute to developing ECM staff leadership and management				
The staff fully understand the relationship between performance management, CPD and sustained improvement in contributing to the learning and ECM well-being outcomes for children and young people				
ACHIEVE ECONOMIC WELL-BEING				
Staff are empowered to be creative and innovative in seeking opportunities to engage children and young people in worthwhile enterprising activities				
Staff CPD related to ECM leads to new and exciting future professional opportunities and potential promotion within the educational setting, EIP and across local networks, clusters and federations				

P *How to Achieve the Every Child Matters Standards*, Paul Chapman Publishing © Rita Cheminais, 2007

HAPTER 6

Monitoring and evaluating progress towards meeting the Every Child Matters Standards

The concluding chapter of this book focuses on the process of monitoring, evaluation and quality assurance in achieving the Every Child Matters Standards award, in order to respond to:

- meeting the requirements of gathering robust and telling evidence on ECM outcomes to support the self-evaluation form (SEF) and the Ofsted inspection process;

- providing evidence to contribute to the single conversation with the School Improvement Partner (SIP), as part of the New Relationship with Schools (NRwS) process;

- providing further evidence for the ECM Standards portfolio, on the educational setting's own self-review of the operational effectiveness of undertaking the entire ECM Standards assessment and award process.

Introduction

Quality assurance (QA) is the process of systematically examining the quality of ECM practice and provision within an educational setting in relation to improving the outputs and ECM outcomes for children and young people. An effective quality assurance system which assesses progress towards meeting expected ECM outcomes is reliant on regular checks and balances through ongoing monitoring and evaluation.

Monitoring is the process of checking progress against objectives or targets set for achieving the ECM Standards identifying any trends, and ensuring that agreed actions and strategies are implemented and that everything goes to plan. Information is gathered from a range of stakeholders and sources, e.g. personal views and first-hand experiences, audit findings, SEF evidence and data collection and analysis, which helps to inform the evaluation process in judging the impact and outcomes of working towards achieving the ECM Standards Award and improving ECM outcomes for children and young people.

Evaluation judges the effectiveness, strengths and weaknesses and interprets how well things are going in relation to impact and outcomes of undertaking the ECM Standards self-evaluation process. Evaluation helps to inform ongoing decision-making and future planning about ECM. It helps to improve ECM practice and to assess whether the educational setting has reached its objective and goal in achieving the ECM Standards Award, and if the ECM outcomes for children and young people have improved. The results of the ECM Standards evaluation need to be reported on and disseminated to stakeholders in an accessible form.

The Ofsted inspection process and the SIP single conversation as part of the New Relationship with Schools (NRwS) provide the external quality assurance health check for ECM in educational settings.

Any educational setting that is engaged in working towards achieving the ECM Standards will be well placed for having gathered sufficient in-depth ongoing evidence of how their ECM policy and provision are contributing to, and impacting on, improving children's and young people's personal development and well-being.

Educational settings will be referring to the ECM Outcomes Framework, the National Service Framework for Children, Young People and Maternity Services, the National Standards for Day Care and Childminding, and the Ofsted inspection framework as national benchmarks for monitoring progress towards improving outcomes for children and young people.

Educational settings are expected to demonstrate value added progress in relation to the five ECM outcomes, particularly in view of them having remodelled their workforce and widened their collaboration with other service providers as part of extended service provision.

Ofsted inspecting Every Child Matters

The educational setting's self-evaluation evidence related to the Every Child Matters outcomes for children and young people is central to the inspection process. The evidence gathered towards achieving the ECM Standards will enable settings to clearly exemplify the impact of actions taken to improve outcomes for children and young people in relation to learning and well-being. The Ofsted self-evaluation form (SEF) specifically evaluates Every Child Matters outcome evidence within Section 3 Achievement and Standards in relation to the ECM outcome Enjoy and Achieve, Section 4 Personal Development and Well-Being and Section 5 The Quality of Provision.

The Ofsted SEF seeks evidence on the following aspects:

- the extent to which learners adopt healthy lifestyles;

- the extent to which learners feel safe and adopt safe practices;

- how well learners achieve and enjoy their learning;

- how well learners are guided and supported;

- how well learners make a positive contribution to the community;

- how well learners prepare for their future economic well-being.

Ofsted, prior to the inspection, via the SEF and any previous inspection report, as well as during the inspection, will seek evidence as to how educational settings, as part of extended service provision, are promoting and improving ECM outcomes.

Ofsted will explore with heads of educational settings:

- what the range and extent of the provision is, how accessible services are and what impact the provision is having on the ECM outcomes for children and young people as learners;

- how the educational setting rates the quality and effectiveness of any integrated care, education and key additional services.

Ofsted will explore with extended service providers:

- what difference and impact the service(s) they provide in educational settings are making to improving the ECM outcomes for children and young people.

(Ofsted, 2005b: 3 and 6).

ECM Standards supporting the School Improvement Partner single conversation

The single conversation with the School Improvement Partner (SIP) that takes place with the leaders and managers in schools and pupil referral units (PRUs) focuses on exploring the answers to the following questions in relation to Every Child Matters:

- how well the educational setting performs overall in relation to Every Child Matters;

- what the strengths and weaknesses are within the educational setting in relation to Every Child Matters;

- what the child/pupil level ECM outcomes data is telling the educational setting and if there are any surprises;

- if there are any trends or issues identified from the educational settings Every Child Matters data analysis that require further attention and how the setting intends to address these;

- whether the educational setting has met all the ECM targets and priorities set on their development plan, and if not how they intend to overcome any barriers that are preventing the ECM targets or priorities from being met;

- how key stakeholders have been engaged in monitoring and evaluating the impact of actions in improving ECM outcomes for children and young people within the educational setting;

- what impact the provision and actions taken by staff from within the setting and from partner providers from other settings and services has had on improving the ECM outcomes for children and young people;

- how the educational setting has monitored and evaluated budget expenditure for ECM provision in relation to ensuring good value for money;

- if there is any further information about ECM that should be included in the school profile or the educational setting's prospectus;

- what the educational setting's future priorities are for Every Child Matters;

- what further external advice, guidance, support and training the educational setting would value and require in relation to moving ECM policy and practice forward.

Participation by the educational setting in working towards achieving the ECM Standards, will provide an excellent source of telling self-evaluation evidence to the SIP as to how the Every Child Matters agenda and outcomes are being addressed within the organisation.

How the ECM Standards support the Ofsted inspection and SIP single conversation

The ECM Standards self-evaluation framework provides educational settings with a robust systematic evidence-gathering process which fulfils the requirements in meeting the various national standards, the SIP single conversation and the Ofsted inspection criteria for Every Child Matters.

The ECM Standards self-evaluation process enables any educational setting to demonstrate clearly:

- what key ECM outcomes have been achieved;

- what impact the educational setting has had in meeting the needs of children, young people and other key stakeholders through its ECM provision;

- how good the quality of the delivery of provision for ECM is in the educational setting;

- how good the leadership and management of ECM is within the educational setting;

- what the educational setting's capacity is for improvement in ECM.
(Adapted from Scottish Executive, 2006: 1–4).

The ECM Standards self-evaluation framework is:

- user-friendly, simple and accessible to use;

- easily navigable;

- fit for purpose to use in a range of different educational settings;

- a positive, reflective, open and cost-effective self-evaluation tool;

- supportive of continuing professional development for ECM;

- helpful in informing future ECM action for improvement.

The value of using the ECM Standards for monitoring and evaluation

The ECM Standards:

- establish an agreed moral purpose and obligation to monitor, evaluate and review the effectiveness of policy and provision on improving children's and young people's learning and well-being outcomes;

- serve the purpose of demonstrating to a wide range of audiences the difference the educational setting is making to the ECM outcomes for children and young people;

- provide a more in-depth quality dimension to the ECM evidence-gathering process;

- measure what is valued in ECM, i.e. capturing 'real stories' about successful ECM outcomes for individual children, young people and their families;

- support a continuous developmental self-evaluation process which promotes a rich ongoing dialogue about Every Child Matters;

- empower a range of stakeholders to contribute first-hand evidence to illustrate the impact and effectiveness of policy and provision on improving ECM outcomes in the educational setting;

- promote and encourage the voice of the child or young person to communicate their views about ECM outcomes in order to inform future improvement.

Using the ECM Standards monitoring and evaluation checklist and reflective review questionnaire

The generic checklist provided in this chapter will help those responsible for monitoring and evaluating an ECM Standard to review the operational effectiveness of the process within the educational setting. The reflective review questionnaire will help to confirm the progress made towards meeting the expected outcomes for each one of the twelve ECM Standards. The person responsible for monitoring and evaluating progress in a particular ECM Standard will be able to cross-check and discuss the information and evidence gathered with the senior staff member leading and overseeing the ECM Standards self-evaluation process throughout the educational setting.

The completed checklist and questionnaire should be included in the ECM portfolio of evidence, with an accompanying overall summary of conclusions and recommendations for further improving the ECM self-evaluation process.

The process of monitoring and evaluating the ECM Standards is designed to be manageable and to involve the minimum of paperwork. The ECM Standards Award process is not over-bureaucratic, as it forms part of everyday practice in relation to self-evaluation for Every Child Matters within the educational setting.

The ECM Standards monitoring and evaluation checklist and review questionnaire in this chapter are also included on the accompanying CD as Microsoft Word documents. Educational settings can add further statements and questions to the checklist and questionnaire as appropriate to suit their particular context. These additional statements and questions may relate to specific, vulnerable groups of children and young people, in relation to the achievement of each ECM Standard.

Points to remember

■ Quality assurance of the ECM Standards provides regular checks and balances through ongoing monitoring and evaluation.

■ Educational settings monitor progress against objectives and targets set on the ECM Standards action plan.

■ Educational settings evaluate the effectiveness of how well things are going in undertaking the ECM Standards self-evaluation and assessment process in order to help inform decision-making and future planning for Every Child Matters.

■ The ECM Standards assist in demonstrating value added progress in relation to Every Child Matters outcomes, which supports meeting other National Standards

ECM STANDARDS OPERATIONAL CHECKLIST

ECM STANDARD: _____

(Place a tick or a cross against each statement to indicate the current position)

- The monitoring and evaluation of the ECM Standards have been built into the educational setting's regular ongoing system of self-evaluation.

- Anyone involved in monitoring and evaluating the ECM Standards fully understands the process and follows agreed procedures.

- The named person responsible for monitoring and evaluating each ECM Standard is known to staff and governors in the educational setting.

- Sufficient non-contact time is allocated in order to allow those monitoring and evaluating an ECM Standard to complete the task successfully.

- Consistent recording procedures have been followed for monitoring and evaluating progress across all the ECM Standards.

- An external critical friend has been commissioned to offer an objective and impartial view on progress made towards meeting each of the ECM Standards.

- Relevant stakeholders, as participants in the process, have been involved in contributing evidence to the monitoring and evaluation of the particular ECM Standard.

- The timescale for feeding back and reporting on the results and outcomes from monitoring and evaluating the ECM Standards has been realistic, clear and adhered to.

- Any monitoring and evaluation reports on each of the ECM Standards, have been produced in an accessible user-friendly format to suit a range of audiences.

ECM STANDARDS PERSONAL REFLECTION AND REVIEW QUESTIONNAIRE

ECM STANDARD: _____

Please complete your responses to the following series of questions and return to the Lead Senior Member of staff for ECM Standards.

1. From the information and evidence gathered for the ECM Standard I have monitored and evaluated, the following trend(s) has been identified:

2. In relation to the ECM Standard I have led within the educational setting, the greatest achievement and outcome for children and young people has been:

3. In relation to the full diversity of children and young people in the educational setting, the cohort or group this ECM Standard has had the greatest impact on has been:

   because:

4. The ongoing evidence gathered for this ECM Standard has identified the following ECM strengths and best practice:

5. The area requiring further improvement and development in relation to this ECM Standard is:

6. The one thing I have gained most from the experience of monitoring and evaluating this ECM Standard has been:

7. When the ECM Standards monitoring and evaluation process is undertaken again, it could be further improved by:

8. The opportunities that monitoring and evaluating this ECM Standard have offered me professionally have been:

9. The greatest challenge that monitoring and evaluating this ECM Standard have offered me professionally has been:

Name: _____ **Date:** _____

Signature: _____

This next question is to be completed by the senior member of staff within the educational setting responsible for leading and overseeing the ECM Standards self-evaluation process.

10. I confirm that sufficient quality information and evidence has been gathered in relation to this ECM Standard.

Name: _____ **Date:** _____

Signature: _____

Appendix – Model materials for use by external ECM Standards assessors

Following on from Chapter 6, model materials are provided for external ECM Standards assessors to utilise with a range of educational settings undertaking the Every Child Matters Standards Award.

These model materials include:

- an information brochure outlining the ECM Standards Award;

- a PowerPoint presentation on the ECM Standards and award process;

- an ECM Standards Award Contract of Agreement;

- an ECM Standards Award Certificate.

These materials are included on the accompanying CD as external ECM Standards assessors are likely to prefer to develop and produce their own ECM Standards support and award materials.

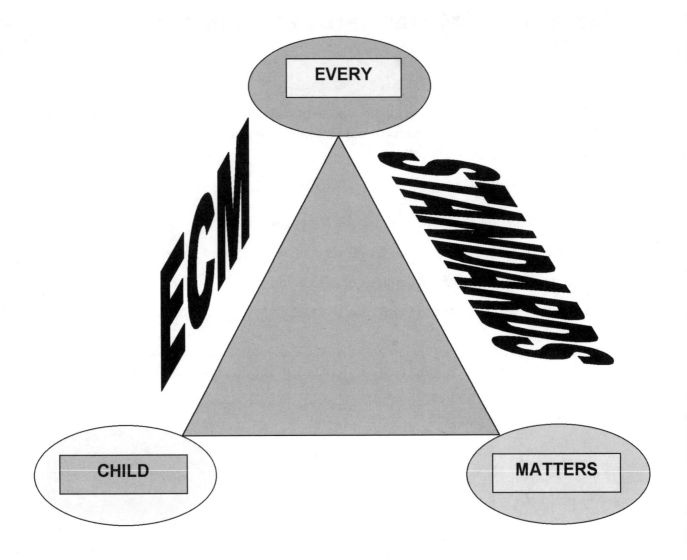

Model Information Brochure

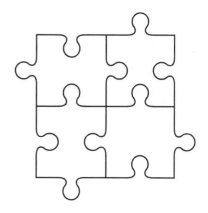

Unclear about where to start on the journey to achieving the ECM Standards Award?

Not sure how all the parts of the ECM Standards self-evaluation process fit together?

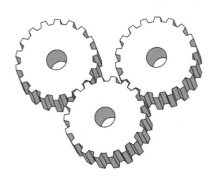

Want to get into gear to begin the journey towards achieving all the ECM Standards?

To find out more about the ECM Standards, read this brochure, and if you think you are ready to begin the journey, then contact the ECM Standards representative for your area.

What are the Every Child Matters Standards?

The Every Child Matters (ECM) Standards are a self-evaluation tool and process that enables any educational setting to judge the quality of its ECM policy, practice and provision against twelve standards and their respective series of outcome evidence descriptors.

†††† Who can participate in the ECM Standards award scheme?

Any of the following educational settings can apply for and undertake the ECM Standards:

- early years settings
- children's centres
- mainstream primary and secondary schools, with or without resourced provisions
- special schools
- pupil referral units
- further education and sixth-form colleges.

What are the advantages of undertaking the ECM Standards process?

- Structure meets the expectations of a twenty-first century Children's Workforce delivering personalised learning and personalised services.
- Aligns with Ofsted inspection requirements and other national quality standards.
- Engages a range of stakeholders as active participants in the ECM self-evaluation process as part of everyday practice.
- Supports ECM capacity building within and across a range educational settings.
- Enables the dissemination and sharing of best ECM practice.
- Offers educational settings external recognition for their good quality ECM policy and practice.

 ## How do you apply for the ECM Standards Award?

Once you have read *How to Achieve the Every Child Matters Standards: A Practical Guide* and have undertaken the initial audit for Every Child Matters, if you consider you are ready to participate in the ECM Standards self-evaluation process, contact the ECM Standards representative for your area to arrange a meeting to discuss the next steps.

P *How to Achieve the Every Child Matters Standards*, Paul Chapman Publishing © Rita Cheminais, 2007

What do you have to do to achieve the ECM Standards?

- Produce an action plan for the ECM Standards, which is kept under review.

- Nominate a senior member of staff to lead and oversee the ECM Standards self-evaluation process.

- Designate a team of staff to gather the ECM Standards outcomes evidence.

- Collect evidence against the twelve ECM Standards to include in a portfolio.

- In agreement with the ECM Standards external assessor, confirm a date for submitting the portfolio of evidence and for the on-site visit to take place.

 ## How long does it take to achieve the ECM Standards Award?

The length of time to achieve the ECM Standards Award is dependent on the educational setting's context. For example, a setting that is a full-service extended school may be well placed to achieve the ECM Standards within a year. Generally, it can take from one year to three years to achieve the ECM Standards Award.

How long is the ECM Standards Award valid for?

The ECM Standards Award is valid for three years. Any educational setting wishing to renew this Award needs to contact the ECM Standards team in their local area to undergo a reassessment.

£ What are the resource implications of the ECM Standards?

Sufficient time needs to be allocated to the lead ECM Standards senior staff member to monitor progress towards meeting the activities set on the ECM Standards action plan. The other staff responsible for collecting evidence for the ECM portfolio will also require enough non-contact time. Supply cover costs for these staff will need to be identified as a resource on the ECM Standards action plan. The ECM Standards assessor will be able to outline in more detail the exact amount of time required to achieve the award in relation to the educational setting's context. They will also outline the costs for consultancy and ongoing support from the ECM Standards team.

How to Achieve the Every Child Matters Standards, Paul Chapman Publishing © Rita Cheminais, 2007

PowerPoint Presentation

EVERY CHILD MATTERS STANDARDS

WHAT ARE THE ECM STANDARDS?

It is a self-evaluation assessment scheme with twelve standards, that if fully met, can lead to an ECM Standards Award

The twelve standards cover:

1. Ethos
2. Policy
3. Environment
4. Leadership & Management
5. Personalised Learning
6. Curriculum entitlement, access and choice
7. Presence, Participation and Personal Development
8. Partnership with parents and carers
9. Multi-agency working
10. The Community
11. Transition & Transfer
12. Professional Development

WHAT ARE THE BENEFITS OF UNDERTAKING THE ECM STANDARDS AWARD PROCESS?

- Involves a range of stakeholders

- Rooted in everyday practice

- Informs the improvement planning process

- Supports and complements the OFSTED SEF

- Supports capacity building for ECM by sharing best practice

- Provides potential for external recognition for ECM policy and practice

WHAT IS INVOLVED IN ACHIEVING THE ECM STANDARDS AWARD?

The ECM Standards self-assessment process entails:

- Undertaking an initial ECM audit

- Preparing an ECM Standards action plan

- Compiling an ECM portfolio of evidence, matched against the twelve Standards

- One-day on-site final assessment visit to observe ECM practice and gather further evidence first hand

How to Achieve the Every Child Matters Standards, Paul Chapman Publishing © Rita Cheminais, 2007

HOW LONG DOES IT TAKE TO GAIN THE ECM STANDARDS AWARD?

- It can take between one year and three years to achieve the ECM Standards Award

- The ECM Standards Award is valid for three years, and can be renewed on reassessment

WHERE AND WHEN CAN THE ECM STANDARDS PROCESS BE UNDERTAKEN?

- Any setting that caters for the personalised learning and well-being of children and young people aged between 3 and 19

- The ECM Standards self-evaluation process can be undertaken by an individual educational setting, or across a cluster, federation or EIP of settings

- It is not advisable to work towards achieving the ECM Standards Award where a setting faces any of the following challenging circumstances: a new build, amalgamation or closure, or is in special measures

WHAT ARE THE PREREQUISITES FOR ACHIEVING THE ECM STANDARDS AWARD?

- There must be a designated senior member of staff to lead and oversee the ECM Standards self-evaluation process within the setting

- A core ECM team needs to be established, comprising between 6 and 12 staff who will each take responsibility for monitoring and evaluating progress in one or two of the ECM Standards

WHO ASSESSES, AND WHERE CAN ONGOING ADVICE AND SUPPORT BE ACCESSED?

- Experienced, knowledgeable senior professionals with a strong background in ECM, commissioned from LA's, HE institutions, educational settings, or independent accreditation companies can act as ECM Standards Assessors and Consultants

- Ongoing advice and support is offered via telephone, email or website

- A scale of charges is set according to the size of the educational setting or the number of organisations participating in a cluster

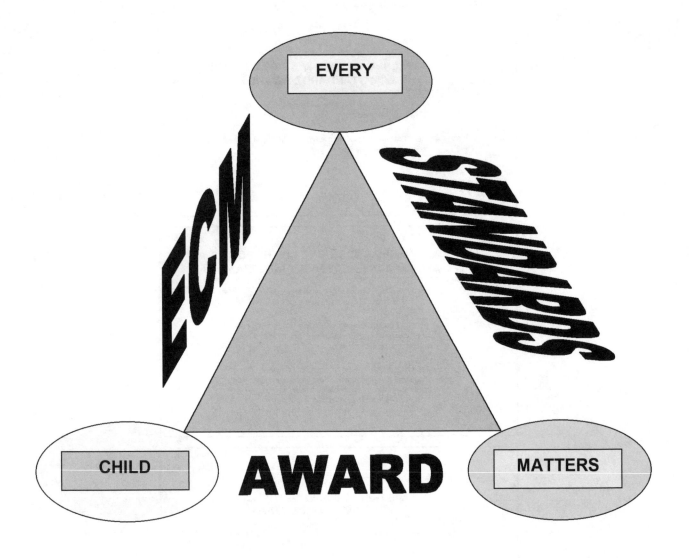

MODEL CONTRACT OF AGREEMENT

This contract of agreement is between _____ and the ECM Standards service provider.

The contract commences on _____ and will terminate on _____

The contract confirms the agreed level of service being provided by the ECM Standards Team to support _____ as the purchasing organisation, throughout the assessment process, which includes:

- an ECM Standards marketing and publicity pack

- an initial planning visit to support the production of the ECM action plan

- INSET session to introduce the ECM Standards process to stakeholders

- ongoing consultancy and support via telephone, e-mail and website

- an interim monitoring review visit

- off-site and on-site moderation and final assessment of ECM evidence

- an Award Certificate to educational settings successfully achieving the ECM Standards.

The purchasing organisation _____ accepts the above service level agreement provided by the ECM Standards Team at a total cost of £ _____ which is payable in full, within 28 days of signing this contract of agreement.

In the event of unavoidable circumstances that prevent the purchasing organisation from completing the ECM Standards in the agreed time, the contract may be renewed for a further twelve months, upon mutual agreement by both parties.

Signature (Head of the Purchasing Organisation): _____

Date: _____   Name (Print): _____

Signature (ECM Standards Service Provider): _____

Date: _____   Name (Print): _____

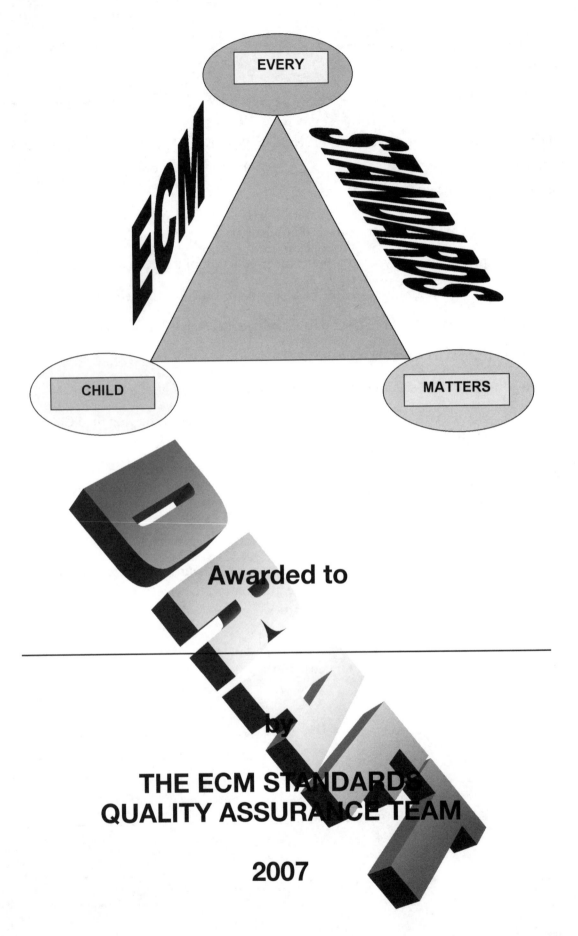

EVERY

ECM

STANDARDS

CHILD

MATTERS

Awarded to

by

THE ECM STANDARDS
QUALITY ASSURANCE TEAM

2007

Abbreviations

AST	advanced skills teacher
CAF	Common Assessment Framework
CD	compact disc
CPD	continuing professional development
CRB	Criminal Records Bureau
DVD	digital versatile disc or digital video disc
ECM	Every Child Matters
EIP	Education Improvement Partnership
HLTA	higher level teaching assistant
HMI	Her Majesty's Inspector
ICT	information and communication technology
INSET	in-service education and training
LAC	looked-after children
LDD	learning difficulties and disabilities
NRwS	New Relationship with Schools
NSF	National Service Framework
Ofsted	Office for Standards in Education
PDF	portable document format
PE	physical education
PRU	pupil referral unit
PSHCE	Personal, Social, Health and Citizenship Education
PSHE	Personal, Social and Health Education
QA	quality assurance
SEF	self-evaluation form
SEN	special educational needs
SIP	School Improvement Partner

Glossary

Additional needs – describes all children and young people at risk of poor Every Child Matters outcomes who require extra support from education, health or social services.

Audit – a systematic and objective overview and review process to compare actual policy and practice against recommended established procedures.

Common assessment framework – a holistic assessment tool used by the Children's Workforce to assess the additional needs of children and young people at the first sign of difficulties who are achieving poorly on the Every Child Matters outcomes.

Distributed leadership – is the distribution and delegation of aspects of leadership across different staff at all levels in order to divide tasks and responsibilities up more equitably.

Early years – refers to children aged 0–7 and their provision in settings such as nurseries and children's centres.

Education Improvement Partnership – involves a group of educational settings collaborating to address the improvement of common issues such as behaviour, 14–19 provision, childcare and extended school provision.

Evaluation – the process of critically examining and judging effectiveness, strengths, weaknesses and how well activities, interventions and initiatives are progressing.

Extended schools – offer a range of core universal services and out-of-hours learning activities from 8 a.m. to 6 p.m. to respond to the needs of children, young people and their families.

Federation – is a group of two or more educational settings, usually schools, which have a formal agreement to work together to improve and raise standards.

Foundation Stage – is a distinct phase of education for children aged 3–5 which provides a framework and curriculum for children's learning and development in nursery and reception classes.

Intelligent accountability – an educational setting's own view of how well it serves its children and young people and its priorities for improvement.

Key worker – is a practitioner from education, health or social care services who provides a lead support and advocacy role for children and young people with more complex additional needs.

Lead professional – is a practitioner from health, social care or education services who acts as a gatekeeper for information-sharing, and coordinates and monitors provision and outcomes for children and young people who have been identified through the common assessment framework process as experiencing difficulties.

Monitoring – is the process of checking progress against set targets in relation to an aspect such as Every Child Matters.

National Service Framework – a set of quality standards for health, social care and some education services aimed at improving the life chances and health of children and young people.

Networking – a collaborative process between staff from education, health and social care services that promotes the sharing of best practice, expertise and resources to support change and innovation.

New Relationship with Schools – is the relationship between self-evaluation and school improvement.

Outcomes – identifiable impact of interventions and services on children and young people.

Personalisation – is where children, young people and their families, as responsible service users, are active participants in the shaping, development and delivery of personalised services.

Personalised learning – entails enabling children and young people to achieve their personal best through working in a way that suits them. It embraces every aspect which includes teaching and learning strategies, ICT, curriculum choice, organisation and timetabling, assessment arrangements and relationships with the local community.

Pupil referral unit – is any centre maintained by an English local authority that provides alternative suitable and appropriate education for children and young people who are not able to attend a mainstream or special school.

Quality assurance – is a form of audit and a systematic examination of quality linked to accountability that ensures a service is of the quality needed and expected by service users.

Safeguarding – describes the process of identifying children and young people who have suffered or who are likely to suffer significant harm and the subsequent action taken to keep them safe.

School Improvement Partner – provides professional challenge and support to leaders in schools and PRUs, to help them to evaluate their performance, identify priorities for improvement and plan for effective change.

Self-evaluation – is a developmental in-depth, reflective, collaborative process at the heart of school improvement, focused on the quality of children's and young people's learning, achievement, personal development and well-being.

Self-review – is a comprehensive overview of selected areas or aspects in an educational setting.

Specialist services – these include services for child protection, adoption and fostering, residential and respite provision, and mental health. These services target children and young people with acute or high levels of need who are at risk of achieving poor Every Child Matters outcomes.

Targeted services – provide support for children and young people with additional and complex needs who are less likely to achieve optimal outcomes.

Transfer – refers to the movement of children and young people from one educational setting or school to another, as in moving from Year 6 in the primary school to Year 7 in the secondary school.

Transition – refers to the move from one year to another within a school or educational setting.

Universal services – or mainstream services, routinely available to children, young people and their families, in and around educational settings.

Vulnerable children/young people – refers to those at risk of social exclusion, who are disadvantaged and whose life chances are at risk. It includes those in public care, children with learning difficulties and disabilities, travellers, asylum seekers, excluded pupils, truants, young offenders, young family carers, and children experiencing family stress or affected by domestic violence.

Wraparound services – provision 'wrapped around' the normal school day which is available through schools, children's centres, nurseries, registered child minders and approved child carers.

Further reading and references

Birmingham City Council Education Service (2002) *Standards for Inclusion: Self-Monitoring for School Improvement*. Birmingham: Birmingham Education Service.

BPEC (2006) *Every Child Matters Unwrapped*. Bradford: Baker-Phillips Educational Communications Ltd.

Cambridge Education (2006) *Making Every Child Matter*, Resource Pack. Cambridge: Cambridge Education Ltd.

Cheminais, R. (2005) *Every Child Matters. A New Role for SENCOs. A Practical Guide*. London: David Fulton.

Cheminais, R. (2006) *Every Child Matters. A Practical Guide for Teachers*. London: David Fulton.

Cheminais, R. (2007) *Extended Schools and Children's Centres. A Practical Guide*. London: Routledge Taylor & Francis.

Coles, C.J. and Hancock, R.M. (2002) *The Inclusion Quality Mark*. Bristol: TLO Ltd.

ContinYou (2005) *How Are We Doing? A Self-Evaluation Toolkit for Extended Schools: The Framework*. London: ContinYou.

CRE (2000) *Learning for All. Standards for Racial Equality in Schools*. London: Commission for Racial Equality.

DfES (2003a) *Every Child Matters*. London: Stationery Office.

DfES (2003b) *Full Day Care: National Standards for Under 8s Day Care and Childminding*. London: Department for Education and Skills.

DfES (2005) *Outcomes Framework – Every Child Matters* (Version 2.0). London: Department for Education and Skills.

DfES (2007) *2020 Vision. Report of the Teaching and Learning in 2020 Review Group*. London: Department for Education and Skills.

DfES/DH (2004) *National Service Framework for Children, Young People and Maternity Services – Executive Summary*. London: Department for Education and Skills/Department of Health.

Haywood, R., Chambers, M., Powell, G. and Baxter, G. (2006) *Ensuring Every Child Matters. Diagnostic and Planning Tools*. Bristol: TLO Ltd.

MacBeath, J. (2006) *School Inspection and Self-Evaluation. Working with the New Relationship*. London: Routledge.

Ofsted (2005a) *Every Child Matters: Framework for the Inspection of Schools in England*. London: Office for Standards in Education.

Ofsted (2005b) *Inspecting Extended Schools*. Briefing paper HMI 2567. London: Office for Standards in Education.

Scottish Executive (2006) *More Than 9 to 4: Out-of-School-Hours Learning in Scottish Education*. Edinburgh: Scottish Executive.

Stubbs, D. (2007) *Auditing Every Child Matters Schools*. Middlesex: Forum Business Media Ltd.

Tutt, R. (2007) *Every Child Included*. London: Paul Chapman.

Index

quality assurance 5, 98, 99
quality assurance check 13
questionnaire, personal reflection and
    review 102, 105

'real stories' 44, 102
records 15
reflection 2
reporting 16
research 2
respect 58, 72

safe practices 99
School Improvement Partner (SIP) 9, 43,
    45, 99, 100–1
secure learning community 2
self-evaluation 9, 10, 11
  data for monitoring ECM 98
  ECM assessment fits in 13
  framework 101
  guiding principles 2
  prompts 42
  regular 45
senior staff 2
shared ownership 2
sixth-form colleges 4

social service practitioners 4
stakeholders 1, 2, 4, 9, 12, 15, 16, 43, 45, 98,
    99, 100, 102
  surveys 44
strengths/weaknesses 15, 43, 99, 100

teachers
  as assessors 4
telephone support 12
terms of reference 2
tolerance 58, 72
transfer 37–8, 66–7, 71, 72, 94–5
transition 37–8, 66–7, 71, 72, 94–5

value for money 101
video 44

website 44
well-being 2, 70, 71, 99
  outcomes 1, 8, 11, 15, 102
wrap around care 9
written evidence 44